SONS OF DUST

SONS OF DUST
THE ROOTS OF BIBLICAL MANLINESS

CHRIS CLEVENGER

© 2015 by Chris Clevenger

All rights reserved. No part of this publication may be reproduced, stored in a retrieval system, or transmitted in any form or by any means without the prior written permission of the author. The only exception is brief quotations in printed reviews.

ISBN-10: 1941972357
ISBN-13: 978-1941972359

Library of Congress Control Number: 2015930912

Published by Start2Finish Books
PO Box 680, Bowie, Texas 76230
www.start2finish.org

Cover Design: Josh Feit, Evangela.com

Unless otherwise noted, all Scripture quotations are from The Holy Bible, English Standard Version®, copyright © 2001 by Crossway Bibles, a publishing ministry of Good News Publishers. Used by permission. All rights reserved.

This book is dedicated to all the men
who have helped initiate and welcome me
into the fullness of biblical masculinity:

My Pops, my Pa, Bill Camp, and others.

Their dedication to Christ and investment
in my life cannot be overstated.

CONTENTS

	Introduction	9
1.	Allow Me to Introduce Myself	13
2.	A World Without Men	23
3.	The Stuff Men Are Made Of	32
4.	The Wonders of Initiation	44
5.	Because It's There	57
6.	The Warrior Within	64
7.	Give Me Liberty	76
8.	The King of the Jungle	86
9.	A Match Made in Heaven	96
10.	The First Poet	107
11.	Have You No Shame?	117
	Acknowledgments	124
	Works Cited	126

INTRODUCTION

We are certainly aware today, at the start of the new millennium, that there is a crisis of manliness in America." When Waller R. Newell penned those words, he could not have been more correct. In every measurable category and at almost every level—the home, the church, the community, the nation, and the world—we are suffering from a lack of complete men. Masculinity has been attacked from without by radical feminism and relativism. The masculine character has also been deteriorating from within, suffering from apathy and a lack of firmness and resolve. Weak men have crippled countless daughters and sons—innocent children reared in homes where they are left without a positive conception of their roles in society. What we need, according to Moore and Gillete, is not "less masculine power. We need more."

But where are we to turn for a clear conception of "masculine power"? A survey of the cultural concept of manliness only produces a smattering of misconceptions amounting to either weak and effeminate men incapable of bearing the burden of leadership, or macho men who embody a cartoonish distortion of real masculinity.

It seems as if we can either find machoism or effeminism—or a weird combination of both. In an attempt to restore real masculinity, some have returned to the Greatest Generation, those who were born out of the war and turmoil of the 40s and 50s; however, as Newell writes, "the search for the manly heart must never be confused with mere traditionalism, a snobbish and sterile veneration of the old way simply because it is old." Most contemporary writers begin searching for the keys to the masculine spirit by studying the current longings of modern men, extrapolating from what they can observe to unlock the hidden heart within every man.

But the roots of real masculinity will never be found by plumbing the depths of the human heart—at least they cannot be found in the heart alone. Our hearts may reveal much to us, but they alone will never accomplish the task. Real manliness can only be found by consulting the One who made man in the beginning. The LORD God is the only One adequately qualified to define what it means to be a man. In order for us to hear from the Creator, we must return to the beginning. We must go back to when God first made man.

We call the first man by a proper name—*Adam*. In the beginning, Adam was simply known as *the Man*. In a very real sense, that is what God created him to be. He was the prototype—the archetype of our kind. By the time God's creative work is finished, He had made the Man to be all that He desired from him. The Man—at least until his fall in the third chapter of Genesis—provides the perfect picture of manliness. Genesis 2 centers upon the character, design, and nature of man more than any other text in all the Bible. In the second chapter of the first book, God pulls back the curtain and shows us a world prepared for man, and the Man prepared by God for the world. He is connected with the earth, for he is made from the dust. Nevertheless, he reigns in dominion over all that God created. He is industrious, driven, passionate, tender, and creative. He is a protector and a provider. He is God's companion and is the counterpart to the crown of God's creation—the Woman. Were it not for the entrance of sin into the world, the Man would have perpetually been the delight of the Lord, living in harmony with Him and exhibiting the nature of God to the rest of the creation.

Any discussion about masculinity, particularly a discussion about biblical masculinity, must be connected with Jesus Christ. The Son of God succeeded where the Man of Genesis failed: Jesus was and is the perfect picture of mature masculinity. He is the "Second Adam." The Man of the Genesis narrative was an image of the coming Christ. During his lifetime, the Son of God presented mature masculinity unlike any the world had ever seen. He was tender, compassionate, and loving. He was strong, courageous, and bold. He lived in a constant dependance upon God that enabled Him to overcome the harshest treatment the world had to offer. In every way, Jesus Christ is the perfect picture of biblical manliness.

We are natural descendants of the first Adam and spiritual descendants of the Second. We are partakers of flesh and blood and heirs of an eternal kingdom. We bear the distinguished title of *Sons of Dust*, for, like our earliest ancestor, we are fashioned from the dust of the ground and connected with the earth that we were made to inhabit. We are also living spirits, endowed with a soul just as Adam was. By returning to the garden in Eden and meditating upon what God created the Man to be, we can be reassured of biblical manliness. We can be taught again by God what He desires from us as men.

What the world needs is real men—men who are being initiated by God and transformed into the image of Christ. We don't need a phycological analysis; we need a spiritual revival. We need to return to the second chapter of Genesis and marvel at the magnificent specimen of mature masculinity that God created in the beginning. We need to see our legacy as Sons of Dust and be reminded that we have been created for a purpose. What God reveals in the Genesis account about mankind is the deepest need for today's society. It will take faith, patience, and the redeeming power of Christ. But we can uncover the roots of biblical manliness. We can be welcomed by Yahweh into His presence as Sons of Dust.

1

ALLOW ME TO INTRODUCE MYSELF

> In the beginning, God created the heavens and the earth.
>
> Gen 1:1

The record of the creation of the first man cannot begin with Adam. Any anthropological study that starts with a complete and living human being presupposes too much and ignores some obvious questions. How did human life originate? Who is responsible for the genesis of man? What was life like for the first of our kind? Besides, a history of man that fails to examine the setting and the players ruins all the mystique and intrigue of the story.

God spoke the universe into creation *ex nihilo*—literally *out of nothing*. He first created light and divided the light from all that remained dark (Gen 1:3-5). On the second day of His creative process, God created an expanse or firmament, dividing the waters on the surface of the earth from the water in the atmosphere (Gen 1:6-8). He caused the bare earth to bring forth vegetation (Gen 1:9-13) and adorned the naked heavens with stars, planets, and comets (Gen 1:14-19) on the third and fourth days respectively. The Lord devoted the fifth day of His creative week to fish and fowl, creatures to populate the skies and the seas (Gen 1:20-23). Cattle, creeping things, and other beasts of the earth were formed on the sixth day of the creative week (Gen 1:24-25).

Before God continued His creative activity, there is a divine pause—a temporary suspension of His supreme prerogative. The text in the second chapter of Genesis calls for us to contemplate the condition of life before Adam. The narrative that begins in Gen 2:4 doesn't start with fish, fowl, birds, and beasts. It doesn't even begin with light. Instead, Moses focuses on the Primordial Cause, the unmoved Mover Himself.

> These are the generations of the heavens and the earth when they were created, in the day that the LORD God made the earth and the heavens.
> Gen 2:4

Man's genesis, the Life that begat his life, is none other than the LORD God Himself. Before we can begin to grasp what it means to be Sons of Dust, we are first moved to marvel at the Designer of us all. We can never grasp what it really means to be a man until we become acquainted with man's Creator. God identifies Himself in three distinct ways as He begins His narrative—through the product of His creative process, His divine activity, and His unique name.

The Genealogy of All Things

The account of the creation of humanity begins like ten other sections in the book of Genesis—"These are the generations" (Gen

2:4; cf. 5:1; 6:9; 10:1; 11:10, 27; 25:12, 19; 36:1, 9; 37:2). This repetitive phrase serves as a dividing point between different narrative texts. Every time the phrase is used, it is accompanied by a name—e.g. Adam, Noah, Shem, Terah—except in the second chapter of Genesis. Here, Moses isn't listing the offspring of a human patriarch; he is recording the birth of the heavens and earth themselves.

God is the Progenitor of all creation, including the human race. He is the One Who designed and created all things in the beginning. "He commanded and they were created" (Ps 148:5). The great and small, the living and nonliving, and the terrestrial and extraterrestrial were all created by divine fiat. All that inhabits the physical realm had its beginning with God. "Worthy are you, our Lord and God, to receive glory and honor and power, for you created all things, and by your will they existed and were created" (Rev 4:11).

Here, even before the creation of Adam, biblical masculinity and common culture reach an impasse. If masculinity is to be defined by culture and society, then we will be led to believe that the proto-man was the result of an initial spontaneous generation and millions of years of natural selection. Any definition of masculinity fashioned upon such presuppositions can only reflect the traits and characteristics traditionally connected with the male gender of our species. Such a definition would have no grounds for assessing what man *ought* to be; it could only compare what man *is* with what man *has been* in the past. In this way, society itself would determine the positive qualities to be associated with masculinity. Successive generations of men have sought to do just that; they have attempted to establish their own criterion for mature masculinity. In doing so, each generation has only done that which was right in their own eyes (Judg 17:6) and has merely managed to establish their own righteousness through a rejection of God's (Rom 10:3).

However, if man is not the result of the evolutionary process and was, instead, created by the hand of God Himself, then the defining of the creation belongs to the Creator. God is the One uniquely qualified to define what it means to be masculine, for He made the male. That which is made is under the authority of the Maker (Rom 9:20-21).

The same divine control that God has exercised over the nations of men (Acts 17:26) is also true of individual men. God created both the sun, moon, and stars and ordained their functions (Gen 1:14-18). He made all biological life, both flora and fauna, and delegated their purposes and qualities (Gen 1:11-12, 20-25). When God created man, he intended for him to fulfill certain purposes, possess particular qualities, and embody the essence of masculinity. The Man was masculine because that is what he was created to be. The foundation of biblical masculinity begins by confidently asserting that God Himself was the Creator of all things.

"I AM WHO I AM"

While the results of the divine creative process are important in and of themselves, their real significance can only be understood when we begin to see Who the Creator really is. We can come to understand a lot about God through His creation—"The heavens declare the glory of God, and the sky above proclaims his handiwork" (Ps 19:1). We can comprehend His majesty, eternality, and supremacy. The heavens and the earth weren't just created by any god; Genesis records that "the LORD God made the earth and the heavens" (Gen 2:4).

THE ROOTS OF BIBLICAL MANLINESS

The Creator chooses to refer to Himself in this section of Genesis in a very interesting way. In Gen 1, He is called *God* (1:1, 3-12, 14). There, God is translated from the Hebrew word *elohim* and is likely used to draw attention to the power of God during the week of creation. Genesis 4 refers to the Father as the *LORD* (Gen. 4:1, 3-4, 6, 9). LORD is the English equivalent of the Hebrew *YHWH* (Yahweh), the covenant name given by God to Moses (Exod 3:14-15). However, in the narrative of the Creation and Fall of man, God is styled as the "LORD God," a combination of both distinguished terms. Moses does not use the terminology again in Genesis and only employs it twice in the rest of the Pentateuch (cf. Exod 9:30; 32:27).

When God reveals the details surrounding the creation of man and the masculine spirit, He chooses to do so as the "LORD God." In so doing, He declares Himself to be both a powerful and personal God.

To say that God is a powerful Being would be an understatement, hence we refer to God as all-powerful. Elohim created the heavens and the earth. He spoke the world into existence (Heb 11:3), and His Son "upholds the universe by the word of His power" (Heb 1:3). God's power is so great that His enemies cower before Him (Ps 66:3). God is solely responsible for the flooding of the entire world (Gen 7:11-24), the destruction of several cities via sulfur and fire (Gen 19:24-25), the drowning of an entire army in the Red Sea (Exod 14:26-29), and countless vanquished kingdoms during the period of the Conquest, judges, and kings of Israel. The boundary of every earthly kingdom has been established by the Lord (Acts 17:26). "The Most High God rules the kingdom of mankind" (Dan 5:21). In the New Testament, the power of God is tantamount to the Gospel of Christ (Rom 1:16). Though Jesus was crucified, it was

Elohim that resurrected Him from the dead. He also ensures our own resurrection (2 Cor 13:4). Salvation—the redemption of man through the blood of Christ—manifests the power of God and far surpasses all mortal wisdom (1 Cor 1:18, 24).

It would not be difficult to imagine that such an infinitely powerful being would remain detached and disinterested in humanity in general. Nonetheless, Moses stresses that Elohim, the omnipotent Creator of the universe, is intimately connected to all of creation, especially man. The second half of the compound name connected to God underlines the personal nature of His relationship with those whom He has made. Our God is a covenant maker; He creates agreements, partnerships, and affiliations with His creation. Yahweh covenanted with Noah, Noah's sons, and all of creation when they disembarked from the Ark (Gen 9:8-17). Abraham entered into a binding agreement with God concerning his heritage and inheritance (Gen 17:1-8). Every Christian is a partaker of a new divine covenant, a superior agreement dedicated by the blood of Christ Himself (Heb 7:22; Matt 26:28). Yahweh makes promises and is serious about keeping His covenants—deadly serious.

The LORD God is not the god of the Deists. He is not disconnected from the affairs of men. He is not a god of the Greeks or Romans—vindictive and often filled with fallibilities and foibles. Nor is Yahweh impotent like the gods of various tribes of people. The LORD God alone is capable of creating man from the dust, establishing a covenant with His creation, and fulfilling His side of the bargain, regardless of drastic changes in circumstances and situations—Satan himself included.

This God—*Yahweh Elohim*—is responsible for the creation of the masculine spirit and all the glorious potential connected to it. As Sons of Dust, we are benefactors of this omnipotent and omnibenevolent God. We marvel at His power and rejoice in His love. I can remember having a similar relationship with my own earthly father. When I was young, I was convinced that my dad was capable of just about anything. When we wrestled, I was powerless before him. But as strong as his hands were, his heart was tender and open to meeting my needs and relating with me as an individual. He was a dependable friend and confidant—one on whom I could rely. In so much as this is true of our earthly fathers, they bear the nature and image of our heavenly Creator.

A God of Action

One of the most common misconceptions about God is that He is entirely inactive. Some believe that He initiated Creation and quietly withdrew to watch history unfold the way we watch an athletic event on television. They mistakenly assume that a lack of miraculous intervention means God is disinterested and motionless. Their god is a god of passivity.

But the LORD God is a God of activity. Genesis 1 reveals that He created, hovered, said, separated, called, made, set, and blessed. Moses records that the Lord is the Cause behind the Creation, the One who "made the earth and the heavens" (Gen 2:4). God says, "I made the earth and created man on it; it was My hands that stretched out the heavens, and I commanded all their host" (Isa 45:12).

The narrative of the creation of man begins by focusing on an active God so that we are not deceived regarding man's form or character. God did not "allow nature to take its course" or suffer mankind to develop all on its own. Such is an impossibility. Instead, the Lord intervened and used the dust which He had created to make man. He formed man's physique and breathed into his nostrils the breath of life. He endowed man with an immortal soul and graced him with a personality. In one sense, the Bible is not a book that records the actions of men; both the Old and New Testaments record the actions of the Creator as He rules history through humanity itself.

The good God is in the detail. God created fingerprints, cells, and atoms. The intricacy and detail of creation is a result of the precise enterprise of the Father. Divine activity is always exact; the creation of man is not different. In his book *Wild At Heart*, John Eldridge recognized this about the nature of God.

> But God made the masculine heart, set it within every man…Now we know God doesn't have a body, so the uniqueness (of Gen. 1:27) can't be physical. Gender simply must be at the level of the soul, in the deep and everlasting places within us. God doesn't make generic people; he makes something very distinct—a man or a woman.

God made something very distinct, very specific. He made the Man and the Woman. Both serve as the archetype of their own lineage. He did not leave their creation up to chance. Nor does he leave us to develop on our own as Sons of Dust. God wants to be involved in the process.

The omniscient, omnipotent, and eternal God fashioned the Man precisely as He intended to. Every detail of his physical, spiritual, emotional, and intellectual self was exactly what God designed. His head, heart, and hands were molded according to God's divine prerogative. Before the Fall, the man was the perfect example of manliness. The man in Gen 2 is only bettered by the Lord Jesus Christ Himself, the second Adam (1 Cor 15:45), for Christ successfully patterned all that God intended for the first man to be—and more. God's activity produced the prototypical man in the ultimate sense.

Machoism or Emasculation

We can never experience biblical manliness without understanding the LORD God. He alone is the unmoved Mover who created the heavens and the earth. Yahweh possesses infinite power capable of all things (Matt 19:26). His divine activity makes a covenant relationship with Him possible and equips us to live the life He has called us to live. He has an interest in mankind and is invested in you. God wrote the book on masculinity—the Bible. He provided us with the Man, a working display, in Gen 2. All that follows—both in the text and in this book—reveals God's intended purpose for man. Sons of Dust look to the narrative of Genesis for insight into their own hearts.

When men try to pursue masculinity without God, they fall into one of two traps—machoism or emasculation. Chauvinism degrades all that is feminine and constructs a masculine caricature. Emasculation so efficiently rejects machoism that even true masculinity is demonized. Neither camp restores true masculinity and both do a disservice to society through the creation of false men who are incapable of filling their needed roles. As Sons of Dust, we reject both extremes and look to God for something greater.

All things began with God. Manliness is no different. Any progress towards manhood must be achieved through a deeper relationship with God. Only God is capable of performing a manufacturer's reset, returning our minds, hearts, and passions to their God-tuned setting.

2

A WORLD WITHOUT MEN

> There was no man to work the ground.
>
> Gen 2:5

A lot of folks have imagined a world without men. Radical feminists have been daydreaming about a world without men—at least in one way or another—since the 1960s. Scientific progress throughout the past two decades has made procreation without the immediate agency of a man a possibility and has provided an avenue for discussions about life without men. Even more recently, *Y: The Last Man*, a science-fiction comic-book series set in a dystopian future, has pondered what a world would be like if all the male mammals on earth were to die.

As discussions about gender roles, femininity, and the general place of men in society are held more often, it becomes increasingly interesting to consider what the world would be like without men altogether.

What would life upon the earth look like without fathers, uncles, sons, or brothers? How would the sciences and arts be effected by the lack of masculine influence? How would school systems, political hierarchies, and communities change to compensate for a lack of the attributes and traits commonly associated with masculinity? How would Christianity itself be different if there were no men?

It might be hard for us to fathom, but God Himself pulls back the curtain and allows us to see what the world was like without men. More specifically, the LORD God shows us the earth before He created man. God created the heavens and the earth (Gen 2:4). After six days of creation He paused and surveyed the realm that He had made. He saw the sun and stars, the freshly created sources of light. God noted the plants, herbs, and vegetation which He had formed on the third day of the creative week. Fish, fowl, creeping things, and all beasts were upon the earth. The only thing lacking from the world was the crown of God's creation—man himself.

> When no bush of the field was yet in the land and no small plant of the field had yet sprung up—for the LORD God had not caused it to rain on the land, and there was no man to work the ground, and a mist was going up from the land and was watering the whole face of the ground.
>
> Gen 2:5-6

Having focused upon God Himself, Moses now directs our attention to a world free of human habitation—a world specifically formed by God for the introduction of man. Moses, like any good author, precedes the introduction of man—the principle character of the second chapter of Genesis—by setting the stage. Like props in a theatrical production, the curtain is pulled away to reveal a world buzzing with life but void of man. Without the Man, the earth was unfinished, unproductive, and unfulfilled.

THE ROOTS OF BIBLICAL MANLINESS

By constructing his story this way, Moses calls for us to pause and survey the scene. We dare not hasten past something which God desires for us to contemplate. There's much to be seen in a world without man and much to be learned about the men that would come to inhabit the silent planet. Like George Bailey in *It's a Wonderful Life*, Sons of Dust need to be shown what the world would be like without their action, productivity, and influence. We need to see a need in order to fill a role.

A World of Potential

On March 2, 2004, the European Space Agency launched a space probe designed for detailed study of the comet Churyumov–Gerasimenko (Comet 67P). After a decade of service, *Rosetta*, as the probe was dubbed, began to orbit 67P in September 2014. Rosetta's lander touched down on the surface of the comet itself on November 12, 2014, becoming the first man-made spacecraft to safely land on a the surface of a comet. Matt Taylor, the Project Scientist for the Rosetta mission, was so excited about the milestone that he called Rosetta the "sexiest mission there's ever been." The scientific community was abuzz with talks of water, amino acids, asteroid mining, and the ever-elusive extra-terrestrial life. Academic and media attention focused upon the mission for one reason—unmeasured possibilities.

Modern-day astronomers, fifteenth-century explorers, and ancient writers were all excited by the same thing—possibilities. When the narrator of Genesis wrote about a world without men, he was inspired to record a similarly exciting situation. The earth before mankind was a world of possibilities created by God. The resources were there; the stage was set for the work of man. God surveyed the entirety of all that He had made and saw a world filled with potential to be realized.

The phraseology employed by Moses in the fifth verse insinuates that God's creative work left ample potential for the industry of man. The area under consideration—the land around Eden—lacked the wild, spontaneous growth of vegetation that followed seasonal rains—the "bush of the field" (Gen 21:15; Job 30:4, 7)—and grains which would later be cultivated by man—the "small plant of the field" (Exod 9:22, 25, 31-32). The reason for the lack of this specific type of wild vegetation is given: God had not caused it to rain. What is interesting is that grains like wheat, millet, and barley would only come in conjunction with the work and labor of man. It would only be through a man's working of the ground that these plants would be produced. There was arable, promising land, but there was no one to work with the elements. No one was there to cultivate and create. There was potential.

Though God's work was good and His creation was magnificent, there were still resources untapped and areas yet to be developed by the creative potential of man. The world was wild, waiting to be dominated by God's image-bearer.

Yahweh has always been a God who sees potential. The Lord saw the potential of Noah when the entire earth was consumed with wickedness. He perceived the great good that a shepherd could do for His people when He chose David as the second king of Israel. Fishermen, tax collectors, rebels, and church-persecutors all had potential as apostles in the service of Christ. Today, the Lord looks at homes, schools, churches, and communities and sees fields that are ready for the harvest (John 4:35). He sees the great potential for masculine influence, leadership, and creativity. Sons of Dust stand in a position to capitalize on the potential placed their by God. "Look, I tell you, lift up your eyes, and see that the fields are white for harvest" (John 4:35). We have a world filled with great potential, ready to be utilized for the glory of God.

A World For Possession

Robert Bly tells an interesting story of perceived possession. A young boy who valued his long, blonde hair was held down and shorn by his father. Emotionally upset and incredibly distraught, the boy sat in the floor until his grandfather took him to the oceanside. The boy and his grandfather stood beside the ocean, and the older man said to the younger, "All this belongs to you." The young boy grew, graduated high school, enrolled in college, and returned to the same shore. The boy, now a man, reflected upon the fact that, though he had changed, what his grandfather had given him remained.

God created the world to be inhabited, to be explored, to be *possessed*. His earliest commands to mankind were, "Be fruitful and multiply and fill the earth and subdue it, and have dominion over the fish of the sea and over the birds of the heavens and over every living thing that moves on the earth" (Gen 1:28). It was God's intention for man to see the same potential divinely built into the creation and to cultivate it. The Creator preinstalled arable land that was suitable for furrowing and farming.

In his book, *Wild At Heart*, John Eldridge writes,

> The secret longing of your heart, whether it's to build a boat and sail it, to write a symphony and play it, to plant a field and care for it—those are the things you were made to do. That's what you're here for. Explore, build, conquer—you don't have to tell a boy to do those things for the simple reason that it is his purpose.

Every man—though some men more keenly than others—knows that he was made to take possession of the world in which he has been placed. When asked why he chose to attempt the ascent of Mount Everest, the tallest mountain in the world, George Mallory is said to have stated, "Because it's there." Mountains were made to be climbed. Rivers were meant to be charted. Seas are there to be sailed.

God didn't create the world to be looked at and nothing more. He created it to be manipulated and worked. The earth isn't an art gallery; it is a laboratory. God intends for us to thoroughly explore and responsibly develop the resources He has placed upon the earth. The manifest destiny of man is to possess what God had given him.

We typically think of possession in one of two ways. A man can be said to possess a thing if he has ownership of it, much like one would own a painting, a knick-knack, or a undeveloped piece of property. However, true possession requires involvement, not just investment. To understand the difference, imagine two men, both of whom have a vast number of books in their home. The first man has thousands of volumes which he bought, placed on a shelf, and never read. The second man bought the books, but then he read them, studied them, and marked them. In one sense both men own impressive libraries, but only the second man truly *possesses* his books.

Sons of Dust have been made to possess the earth. We weren't created to be Little Hitlers; far from it. We were made to enjoy the earth God has placed under our dominion. The mountains are His, but He has given them to us as an inheritance. All of creation—though much of it is incredibly wild—was created for the Man. The world was created to be possessed by man, to be used industriously in service unto God.

A World For Partnership

What amazes me about man's role in the world is that God has seen fit to include mankind in the creation and cultivation of the world at all. God is sufficiently powerful to fashion the world just as He desires. If He spoke the world into existence, then He can certainly manipulate the elements according to His will. In fact, both the Father and the Son have done so repeatedly throughout history. Nevertheless, the LORD God determined to work with and through man in the process of the cultivation of the earth.

There were no wild, growing plants or cultivated grains. Why? Because there was a lack of rain, and there was no cultivator. God solved the lack of moisture by providing a regular source of moisture over the face of the earth (Gen 2:6). Whether it was a mist, a subterranean spring, or actual regular rainfall (Job 36:27) is of little importance. What is significant is that God chose to do a part and leave the rest to the industry of man.

Several weeks ago, I was splitting wood on a friend's farm in western Tennessee. After several hours of working alone, Micaiah, a two-year-old boy, came outside to get involved. His mother was thankful that I didn't hand him the axe and turn him lose. Instead,

I handed him a small limb to stack with the rest of the wood which had already been split. I did most of the work and allowed Micaiah to do what he could do.

God operated with the Man—and He still works with us—in a similar fashion. The first man could not control the weather patterns, the seasons, or the overall climate of the earth; however, the Man that God would create could plow the ground and plant the seed. The Man could cultivate the earth. God would do His part by providing the rain in its time; man would do his part by working the ground. In this way, God entered into a partnership with man.

This isn't the only time God chose to work with and through men. He chose Abraham, Joseph, and Moses. He worked through Joshua, the judges, and the kings. Later in the New Testament period, Christ would choose to enter into a coalition with the apostles to spread the message of the Gospel (Mark 16:15-16). As the LORD God, Yahweh rules history with and through chosen humanity.

Man, if he is as God has intended him to be, does not only work *for* God. Real men work *with* God. Men work with God in the home, leading their wives and children to deeper levels of relationship with God. Men labor alongside God in the community by developing order and harmony, instead of allowing chaos. Even on the job, men work with God by using mental prowess, industry, and work ethic to develop and create.

A World For the Taking

A world without men is a world for the taking. Before God created the Man, the world was filled with potential and ready for the partnership of God and man to truly possess it. It was there—bold and wild—and was ripe for the picking. The Sons of Dust live in a world populated by shadow men, mannequins parading as men. This world of fakes is a world that needs real masculinity. There is so much potential to be realized, so many raw resources to be cultivated, centered, and utilized to glorify God. However, real men will never be able to conquer this world alone. Any attempt to do so will deteriorate into a base pursuit of power unless it is centered upon God Himself. The Sons of Dust do their best work—the only real work they ever will do—in a deep, real partnership with God. We work hand-in-hand with Yahweh.

3

THE STUFF MEN ARE MADE OF

> What is man that you are mindful of him, and the son of man that you care for him?
>
> Ps 8:4

When I was a boy, I was told that little girl were made of sugar, spice, and everything nice. On the other hand, boys were made of snips, snails, and puppy dog tails. Not taking the limerick literally, we understand that there is something profoundly different about the make-up of men and women, even when they are extremely young. Men are from Mars, and women are from Venus. Men are like waffles, and women are spaghetti. Men are microwaves, and women are crockpots. Need we say more? In the old rhyme, we connect maleness with construction and destruction, zoology, and canine anatomy; but, on a deeper level, we understand that man is made of much more.

John Eldridge wrote, "If a boy is to become a man, if a man is to know he is one, this is not an option. A man has to know where he comes from, and what he's made of." We need to understand our composition; our mettle needs to be tested. We need to be familiar with who we are, what we are, and what we were created to be.

When Moses records the creation of man in Gen 2, he does so in remarkable detail. Very little is said about the creation of the universe. Planets, stars, and whole galaxies are made without receiving any special type of attention; however, when the trinitarian God begins to fashion man, Moses records the entire process, carefully directing attention to the making of man.

> Then the LORD God formed the man of dust from the ground and breathed into his nostrils the breath of life, and the man became a living creature.
> Gen 2:7

This revelation about the creation of the Man implies a lot about us, and we are uncomfortable with some of those things. Man was made by the divine hand of God and fashioned exactly to His specifications. He was made from dirt—a substance that permeates every place on earth. God is the source of our life, but the dust of the ground is the substance from which we are made. We're made in His image, by His hand, and for His purpose. Yahweh wanted us to be introduced to our own creaturely dependence upon Him and our spiritual connection with the divine.

Humility

As we've already established, God created all things *ex nihilo*; but when it came time to make man, God chose to use something He had already created to fashion the first man—dirt. The Lord created light and the foundations of the earth instantaneously and from nothing, but man was made with the dust of the ground.

We often associate rarity with worth. Gold, silver, plutonium, and diamonds are only considered valuable when they are rare. Were there a world where diamonds were as common as rocks, it would be hard to imagine that they would be highly valued at all. For that reason, we don't place a lot of importance upon dirt or dust. It's common, covers the surface of the earth, and fills every crack and crevice in our homes. We dust our homes, wash our clothes, and bathe to rid ourselves of it. However, dirt has a way of worming its way back into our lives. In this way, the common, everyday dust we try to avoid has a way of reminding us of the simple and humble roots of our earthly existence.

Ernst and Walter Jacob notice that the soil is man's "cradle, his home, and his grave." We came from dust, live with dust, and will return to the dust. Everything about our earthly existence is earthly—save for the spark of the divine place within us. Man's relationship and commonality with the dirt is even expressed in the words that Moses wrote to refer to each. The Man is *adam*; the ground is the *adamah*. Man is intimately connected to the ground, the same earth that he was made to till (Gen 2:6). Ninety-nine percent of your body is composed of six incredibly common elements: oxygen, carbon, hydrogen, nitrogen, calcium, and phosphorus. As far as the elements themselves are concerned, there is nothing remarkable or rare about the human body. It would be difficult to be more common on a chemical level.

It makes us uncomfortable to connect ourselves with such humble origins, but the Bible does so again and again. After the Fall,

God told Adam that he was taken from the dust and would return to the dust (Gen 3:19). "I am dusts and ashes" were words spoken by Abraham. Job was made like clay and would return to the dust upon death (Job 10:9; 34:15). The Preacher knew we all came from the earth and would there return (Eccl 3:20). God "knows our frame; he remembers that we are dust" (Ps 103:14).

Our connection with the dust of the earth produces humility. We are reminded of our feeble nature, our human foibles, and our repeated failures. We recognize our lowly position, especially in relationship to an infinite Creator. When biblical characters cover themselves with dust and ashes, they portray the humility and lowliness of our dirty creation.

In order for a boy to become a man—a biblical man—he must take on a journey of humility. The spiritual giants of the past all recognized the essentiality of a humble spirit before God. Our God "opposes the proud, but gives grace to the humble" (Jas 4:6). "Whoever exalts himself will be humbled, and whoever humbles himself will be exalted" (Matt 23:12).

In their book about mature masculinity, Moore and Gillette write that "the key to maturity, to moving from Boy psychology to Man psychology, is to become humble, to be grasped by humility." Every man must take a katabasis; he must descend in order to become what God desires for man to be. Some men descend voluntarily. Jesus Christ is the epitome of this type. He "emptied Himself by taking on the form of a servant" and "humbled Himself by becoming obedient to the point of death, even the death of the cross" (Phil 2:5-8). John Eldridge notes that Jesus, "the master of wind and sea, lived in a desperate dependence on his Father." Men who choose the path of self-imposed humility recognize their composition and submit voluntarily to God. Other men are forced into humility. Kings were humbled by God's judgment. Job was humbled by suffering. Joseph was humbled by the circumstances of life. Men can be guided into humility by poverty, sickness, or a loss of position and power. The humble situations of these men can be the result of divine intervention or subconscious self-destruction. Robert Bly rightly noted that "the state of being 'discharged' is a good and holy state that prepares for the Descent." Every masculine journey begins with humility; every biblical man knows his own limitations.

You have a choice to make: you will either humble yourself, or you will be humbled. If you humble yourself, God will exalt you in the proper time (1 Pet 5:6). Those who refuse to bow before their Creator in lowliness will be brought low—whether in this life or the next. We either learn to shudder now or will forever tremble in eternity.

Spirituality

As God was forming man from the dust of the ground, there came a point where the physical construction of the body was complete. Under the hand of the Almighty was a perfect specimen physiologically. Bare skin concealed a divinely sculpted muscular system. A perfect heart was buried within the chest of the man; veins and arteries permeated the whole. Eyes rested in their sockets, every organ was present, and the brain was intact. But at the same time, there was no steady rise and fall of respiration. The eyes were lifeless and empty. No heartbeat could be heard resounding in the chest of the corpse.

This should give us pause. This sculpture of dust was dead without what God bestowed next. There is little difference between a body with life and one without. In the same way, there is little physical difference between a man who has life and one who does not. The invisible contribution of God brings life. Our story reveals that, after having constructed man from the elements, God "breathed into his nostrils the breath of life" (Gen 2:7). Only after the breath of God entered the lifeless lungs did the Man live. He was not resuscitated, revived, or rejuvenated; the man was not given life *again*, but blessed with life for the first time. Without God's divine activation, the Man would have never lived.

It is interesting that the breath of God provided the impetus for the life of man. Like a blacksmith nursing a bed of coals, God kneels beside the man and blows into his nostrils. His heavenly breath fans the flames of human existence and causes the dust to live. The Man's lungs contracted and relaxed. His heart began to beat. He was alive for the first time. Later in the Old Testament, God instructed one of his prophets to engage in a similar activity. Ezekiel was told to command the wind to breathe upon a collection of lifeless bodies already constructed by prophetic utterances (Ezek 37:7-10). Ezekiel did the same thing in the Valley of Dry Bones that God did outside the garden in Eden. In both cases, the breath of God provides life.

The life bestowed by God was certainly physical. Like the beasts of the field, God's breath made man a living creature, one who possesses the "breath of life" (Gen 7:15, 22). We could say that this aspect of man's life is natural, consistent with the rest of nature. Birds and beasts, cattle and crows have this type of life. However, God's special activity during the creation of man implies that more than physical life was bestowed.

Man is unique among God's creation. Mankind alone has an eternal soul. Animals and vegetation possess life, but man is unique in that he has a soul. Man was given not only natural life but supernatural life—spiritual life. God formed man from the dust of the ground and planted a soul within him (Ecc 12:7).

Any approach to masculinity that covers only the physical and material side of man is entirely incomplete. Manliness involves more than muscles and mental acumen. Biblical masculinity is deeply concerned with the spiritual aspect of man. Since man is a spiritual being he needs spiritual activity. Were man only natural, he would need only physical sustenance—food, fire, water, and shelter. However, since man is a spiritual being, he needs something more. He needs a deep connection with God and the nourishment for his soul that only God can provide. "My soul clings to the dust; give me life according to Your word!" (Ps 119:25).

The Bible describes the fulfillment of the spiritual needs of man as an ongoing relationship or walk with God. Adam walked with God in the Garden of Eden (Gen 3:8), Enoch walked with God (Gen 5:24), and Abraham was the friend of God (Isa 41:8). Moses talked with God face-to-face (Exod 33:11). Christ constantly communed with His Father. Every Biblical man throughout the history of the earth has been intimately connected with God. John Eldridge writes, "Adam, Abraham, Jacob, David, Jesus—they all learned who they were out of their intimacy with God, with the Father." Pascal noted that there is a God-shaped void in the heart of every man. Material and physical things alone cannot fill such a hole. Only God

Himself can satisfy the deep longing of man's heart. If we are going to pursue biblical masculinity, then we must seek God Himself. Our humility—the katabasis connected with man's earthiness—moves us to connect with the Creator. When such a connection takes place, man is shaped by the Spirit of God, and the mature traits of Christian masculinity are cultivated. Without a spiritual connection with God, and apart from the polarizing concepts of revelation, masculinity becomes a degenerate corruption of what God intended.

God's original intent was for masculinity to be created, cultivated, and consummated in His presence. Much like Adam thrived in the presence of God in the garden, true masculinity is only achieved and maintained through a daily relationship with God. Today, that relationship is only found through Christ. In their book, *A Guide to Biblical Manhood*, Stinson and Dumas highlight the idea that "mature manhood was forged in the body of Christ." We are cleansed from sin and added to the body of Jesus—the church—by the blood of Christ (Acts 2:38, 47; Gal 3:26-27). In the church, we have access to God and walk in fellowship with Him (1 John 1:7). In the church we are molded by the Holy Spirit (Gal 5:22-23), sharpened by the community faithful men (Prov 27:17), and enjoy spiritual blessings and fulfillment (Eph 1:3).

The breath of God imparted life—both physically and spiritually. Manliness is created and sustained through an intimate relationship with the Creator. Humility and spiritual connection intertwine to create the complete man.

Man's Dual Nature

It would be helpful at this juncture to discuss the apparent dualism of man. Some have tried to divide man's nature into at least two different categories—the physical and the spiritual. It is easy to see how such a conclusion can be reached. Man was created from the dust, a physical construction, and then endowed with a living soul. However, any view of man that divides him in two separate and distinct parts is not entirely biblical. Moses does not present two opposing halves of the Man in the second chapter of Genesis. Instead, the first man is created as a united being. The body was not evil and the spirit good, for God pronounced all to be good after it was created (Gen 1:31). The body without the spirit is dead (Jas 2:26); the spirit without the body is incomplete—at least as far as man is concerned.

That last statement may seem strange, but consider what Paul writes in 1 Cor 15. When the second coming of Christ takes place, the souls of the saints shall be reunited with their bodies, those bodies will be changed, and immortal bodies of some form will enjoy eternity with God (1 Cor 15:50-53). Between death and the resurrection, man is incomplete. Something is missing that God intended for him to possess—a body.

If such is the case, then any understanding of biblical masculinity must encompass the totality of the unified man—both his spiritual and his physical being. God created the Man so that his physical existence would be enriched and ennobled by his spiritual being. On the other hand, the spiritual life of the first man was deepened and expressed through the physical. The spirit is not pitted against the body ascetically, nor is the body embattled against the spirit.

What of the flesh? The flesh—the physicality of man—is not sinful in and of itself. When the desires of the flesh are left unchecked by the spiritual part of man, then they are sinful. Hunger—a physical desire—is not sinful. But when it is polluted, hunger becomes gluttony. The sexual desire of man is certainly physical but not sinful itself; such desire is sinful if it is directed and expressed outside of spiritually acceptable boundaries. The flesh must be subordinate to the spirit (1 Cor 9:27). After all, man was not a living being until the spirit was added to the body itself. Likewise, the body without the spirit is dead, though the spirit may live without the body.

Plato employs an interesting illustration in his dialogue with Phaedrus. He describes a chariot being pulled by two winged horses, one white and the other black. This picture—one commonly used throughout history—presents the charioteer as driving the pair of horses by keeping them in harmony one with the other. In this illustration, man would be the charioteer and the horses would represent the spiritual and physical aspects of man's nature. Every man is responsible for guiding his own chariot by keeping his fleshly desires reigned in and directing both horses towards God Himself. The biblical man places the spiritual horse in the lead, subjecting the black horse to his command. From time to time, the black horse of the flesh and the white horse of the spirit will pull against one another (Gal 5:17). If man allows the fleshly side of his nature to lead him, then he will be led astray and will die (Gal 6:8). But if he follows the Spirit, he will live abundantly (John 10:10).

Dust and Deity

When God made man, He made both a body and a spirit. The body, that part made from dust and subject to corruption, drives us to humility. We bow before our Creator and acknowledge our frailty and dependance upon Him. We contemplate our spirit and recognize that we were made for more than physical endeavors. We were created to have a deep, meaningful, and lasting relationship with God Himself.

When humility and spirituality are connected, we truly begin to live. Biological life without spiritual life is really death (Eph 2:1-3). Biblical masculinity brings together these two aspects of man and unifies them for the glory of God. God created you to live for and with Him. By directing all that you are God-ward, you'll be able to enjoy the virility only known through biblical manliness.

I love to run alone in the woods. It gives me time to spend reflecting and communing with my Creator while enjoying all that He has given to me. There's something incredibly exciting about pushing your physical limits while maintaining an ongoing conversation with God. I've never felt more alive than when running through the woods in the pouring rain. One summer afternoon, I went out for a trail run through a local state park. As I descended into the woods, it started to rain. I considered turning around and calling off my excursion, but something within spurred me to keep going. I offered up a prayer and picked up the pace. Snaking around trees, splashing through puddles, and sliding on wet mud has a way of making a man feel alive. I let out a holler, prayed out loud, and had one of the best experiences of my life. I was able to unite my body and soul in one activity—a run with God through a quiet wood.

True biblical manliness repeats the same process every day by connecting our physical challenges and achievements with the Father of spirits. Men aren't made of snips, snails, and puppy dog tails alone; real men are a mixture of dust and deity.

4

THE WONDERS OF INITIATION

O God, from my youth you have taught me, and I still proclaim your wondrous deeds.

Ps 71:17

We now arrive at an important juncture on our journey to masculinity. We have been introduced to the LORD God, the One who created the earth and the heavens and who desires a creature with whom to relate. He has shown us a world prepared for men. This world is filled with potential—there are mountains to be climbed, gardens to be tilled, and beasts to be subdued. The earth is ripe for the taking, as long as the Man is willing to work with God to accomplish his tasks. We knelt beside Yahweh and watched as He formed the Man from the dust and gave him life. As we beheld God's work, we were humbled and connected with a God who is spiritual and has created us to be spiritual as well. But there is still so much to be learned. The Man now stands beside the Lord and waits for direction. He needs to be taught. The Man needs to be initiated. We too need to be initiated.

Robert Moore and Doug Gillette rightly acknowledge the need for masculine initiation in their book about the archetypes of mature masculinity.

> It can be said that life's perhaps most fundamental dynamic is the attempt to move from a lower form of experience and consciousness to a higher (or deeper) level of consciousness, from a diffuse identity to a more consolidated and structured identity. All of human life at least attempts to move forward along these lines. We seek initiation into adulthood, into adult responsibilities and duties toward ourselves and others, into adult joys and adult rights, and into adult spirituality.

Initiation, though it has been completely neglected by the populace at large during the 21st century, serves as one of the foundational prerequisites to positive, mature masculinity. John Eldridge writes, "Masculinity is bestowed. A boy learns who he is and what he's got from a man, or the company of men. He cannot learn it any other place." When the Man began to be, he needed to be taught by God, the source of all true masculinity. We know why the Man was created—to cultivate the ground (Gen 2:5). However, he did not know until he was told. God decided to show the Man the task for which he had been created.

> And the LORD God planted a garden in Eden in the east, and there he put the man whom he had formed. And out of the ground the LORD God made to spring up every tree that is pleasant to the sight and good for food. The tree of life was in the midst of the garden, and the tree of the knowledge of good and evil.
>
> Gen 2:8-9

In a very real sense, God initiated Adam. Moore and Gillette identify two necessary prerequisites for a successful initiatory process, what they call "sacred space and...a ritual elder." In the account of the creation of man recorded by Moses, we find these two and another equally important aspect of initiation—instruction. All three of these are present in Gen 2:8-9. God—the ritual Elder—initiated the Man by placing him in a specially prepared haven—sacred space—and demonstrating the process of cultivation necessary to work the garden—instruction.

When we consider that the Man needed to be initiated, it makes since that God waited to plant the garden of Eden until after the creation of man. The Man had none other to teach him about plowing, planting, or planning. He had never seen the earth cultivated, nor beheld a single piece of farming equipment. The Lord planted a garden, placed the man in the perfect paradise, and produced plants for sustenance. Through this initiatory process, the LORD declared His desire for man and helped a conscious collection of dust become a mature man. Through God's active intervention, He not only created a man physically and spiritually, but He cultivated manliness emotionally and psychologically.

Each of these aspects of initiation—sacred space, the ritual Elder, and instruction—is worthy of a deeper mediation.

Sacred Space

In the Genesis account, God made a man and caused him to stand upright. The Man was given all the qualities and abilities necessary to fulfill his God-given function. He was physically mature, endowed with the strength and virility necessary to "fill the earth and subdue it." The Man was a spiritual creature capable of ongoing fellowship and communion with God. The Man was also an intelligent and creative being—as we will notice later.

Now that the Man had been created, God began to create a home for him. He chose a suitable portion of land in the East, an area of the ancient world connected with fertility and bounty. For His son, the viceroy of His creation, God would provide nothing but the best. The name given by Moses to the area where God chose to create man's habitat was *Eden*—a delightful or happy land. God constructed a garden within a portion of the land of Eden. This garden—the *paradiso*—was an enclosed area intended for cultivation. The garden planted by God was a paradise—a haven where the Man could commune with his Maker. This type of garden was popular with royalty in the Ancient Near East, especially the Persians and Babylonians. The Hanging Gardens of Babylon, one of the Seven Wonders of the Ancient World, were built by Nebuchadnezzar II as a haven for his Median wife and serve as an example of such. God's construction of a perfect garden home for the Man demonstrated His love, care, and interest in Man's wellbeing.

There is much that we don't know about the garden in Eden. Bible students and historians have tried in vain to pinpoint its exact location. In doing so, they have failed to see the import of the garden itself to the narrative. Eden isn't important because of where it is. The paradise prepared by God is of great significance because of what takes place there. In Eden, God constructs a sanctuary where the Man can be initiated and enjoy harmony and fellowship with God. Before the creation of the Woman, the Man, and the LORD were alone in sacred space. They were able to enjoy an intimate fellowship that provided man with skills, resources, and information that he would later need to be a good husband, father, and steward of the earth.

The garden of Eden was the sacred space prepared by God for Adam's initiation. A mountain in the Arabian peninsula was chosen for Moses. The Valley of Elah severed as David's sacred space, though his initiatory process probably began in the fields while tending sheep. Saul of Tarsus was spiritually initiated in the wilderness. Each of these men were taken to a sacred place, a place where they could be initiated and transition into mature Biblical masculinity.

Sons of Dust today are in need of initiation. We need to be ushered into adulthood. Thousands of American men teeter aimlessly between childhood and adulthood in an extended state of adolescence. Society in general has done a poor job of "making men." Our rejection of ritual initiation and our lack of a well-defined transition from childhood to adulthood has drastically shrunken the pool of contributory men in homes, communities, churches, and even in the work force. We need a sacred space for initiation, but where can such a location be found when much of the surface of the earth has been charted, tamed, and declared wholly unholy? The space alone, or rather the geographical location of such a space, is not determined naturally. For space to be declared sacred, Someone must be present.

The Ritual Elder

What made the garden of Eden sacred space? Why was it the special spot of initiation for the Man? It was sacred because God was there. Where the Lord walks is holy ground (Exod 3:5; Josh 5:15). Never had an initiation taken place before. Never had God isolated man from the rest of creation. Here, in the garden in Eden, Yahweh separates man and begins to introduce him to the responsibilities and tasks for which he was created. It is the divine presence of God that makes the garden of Eden a sacred place. Were God absent from the garden, it would have been a botanical home void of a meaningful initiatory process. The garden of Eden without God would have been nice to look at, but would not have produced a fully mature man. The Man needed the LORD to make the transition possible.

Since masculinity is bestowed, someone—or rather Someone—needed to bless the newly formed Man. Bly writes, "The ancient societies believed that a boy becomes a man only through ritual and effort—only through the 'active intervention of the older men.'" In the initiation of the first man, God serves as the ritual Elder and Intervener in the life of Adam. We cannot be sure what the Man would have become had the Lord never provided the necessary environment for his transition into the fullness of manhood, but we can be sure that it would not have been along the same lines as what was developed by God. Man would have had no purpose, direction, and certainly no spouse. All of the trappings associated with mature masculinity were provided and unveiled by God through the process of initiation.

Why did God Himself initiate the Man? There was no one else present to do so. Furthermore, who would be better suited to pass intelligence, purpose, and direction on to man than the Creator of man? Later, with the birth of subsequent generations of male children, the initiatory responsibility would be shared by older men;

however, these older men could only introduce boys to biblical masculinity by connecting them with the true Father. In one sense, this implies that initiation involves three different parties—the boy being initiated, the man who is performing the initiation, and God Who oversees and directs the other two parties. Take, for example, the initiation of the apostles under Jesus Christ. The apostles—all twelve—were the subjects of initiation, Christ was the immediate Initiator, and the Father was involved in the entire process. So intimate was the Father's involvement that Jesus prayed to Him before the selection of the Twelve (Luke 6:12-13) and then for the apostles at the conclusion of His earthly ministry (John 17). Place that in contrast to modern initiation by fraternities. Frat houses often subject would-be brothers to cruel initiation ceremonies and then, assuming pledges achieve the required parameters, are welcomed into "brotherhood." However, fraternities are completely incapable of producing real masculinity. In order for anyone to be initiated into mature biblical manliness, God must be the impetus and focus of the process.

When a boy is placed into sacred space and spends intimate time there in the presence of God, then it is possible for him to be initiated. Eldridge writes, "Adam, Abraham, Jacob, David, Jesus—they all learned who they were out of their intimacy with God, with the Father." These great heroes of the faith all learned who they were and what they were destined to be by communion with God. Elders of the church, older Christian men, and fathers can play a valuable role in initiating younger males into biblical masculinity. By placing them in position conducive to spiritual growth, serving as teachers and guides in biblical matters, and through patterning biblical manliness intentionally, mature Christian men can serve as a connection to God and provide a catalyst for initiation.

Once we are in the presence of God—in sacred space—we can begin to comprehend what God desires of us. We are given the opportunity to be taught by God Himself.

Instruction

The ninth verse of Gen 2 specifies the process that God used when He planted a garden in Eden. Moses says that the Lord "made to spring up every tree that is pleasant to the sight and good for food." Two trees are specified—the Tree of Life and the Tree of the Knowledge of Good and Evil. What God was allowing was for the Man to see the industry, creativity, and providence associated with masculinity itself—or, in the ultimate sense, Masculinity Himself. The Father brought His first son to the job site and explained what he was made to do. Robert Bly rightly recognized the value of a father teaching his son how to work when he wrote,

> The traditional way of raising sons, which lasted for thousands and thousands of years, amounted to fathers and sons living in close—murderously close—proximity, while the father taught the son a trade ... the love unit most damaged by the Industrial Revolution has been the father-son bond.

The Man, present with God when He created man's garden home, received a valuable education from the Creator. Through the constructive process, the LORD revealed three things about mature masculinity that must be grasped to fulfill initiation. God connected each of these three things with a specific type of plant that He brought forth in the garden.

First, the LORD God caused visually stimulating plants to come from the earth. Our text says that these plants were "pleasant to the sight" (Gen 2:9). It is interesting that the cultivation of beauty is mentioned before the other plant life. God connects artistic expression and creativity with Himself and the Man. We typically associate beauty, loveliness, and creative expression with the feminine; however, such a notion is a relatively recent phenomenon and is to our own discredit. Many of the most creative minds throughout history have been incredibly masculine. Michelangelo, Einstein, and even Churchill were known for their creativity. David is exalted as a creative conqueror, both the champion and sweet singer of Israel (cf. 1 Sam 16:23; 17:48-51). Jesus Christ, the God-man, was both the creator of all things (John 1:1-3) and the captain of our salvation (Heb 2:10). According to Bly,

> The job of the initiator ... is to prove to the boy or girl that he or she is more than mere flesh and blood. A man is not a machine only for protecting, hunting, and reproduction ... [he] carries desires far beyond what is needed for physical survival.

In initiation, the Man learned that God's desire for him was that he express himself creatively in the world around him. Art, poetry, mathematics, architecture, music, and even law are demonstrations of this creative process. When we as men engage in these activities, we are connecting ourselves with a heritage begun by God Himself.

Second, the Lord planted and produced trees and plants that were good for food. These are logically linked with the "small plants of the field" that had not yet sprung up (Gen 2:5). As a Father, God is teaching our forefather both the necessity of providing for yourself and others, and the process by which such providence is made. More will be said about work and work ethic later in the narrative, but it suffices us to say here that God is demonstrating one of the chief obligations of masculinity—the requirement that a man provide for his family. If any man "does not provide for his relatives, and especially for members of his household, he has denied the faith and is worse than an unbeliever" (1 Tim 5:8). Furthermore, "If anyone is not willing to work, let him not eat" (2 Thes 3:10). A biblical man provides for the needs of himself and his family by using the skills, abilities, and resources God has placed under his dominion.

Third, and probably most significantly, God highlighted the Man's spiritual needs by planting two special trees in or around the garden in Eden. According to Moses, God planted the tree of life in the midst of the garden. Somewhere nearby, we presume, God planted the infamous tree of the knowledge of good and evil. These two trees served an even greater purpose than providing physical nourishment or visual stimulation. These two trees served to teach the Man that he had spiritual needs and requirements.

The tree of life imparted perpetual life to all those who partook of its fruits (cf. Gen 3:22-24). This tree is figuratively said to be planted in the paradise of God, heaven itself (Rev 2:7), and is connected with wisdom (Prov 3:18). On the other hand, the tree of the knowledge of good and evil is mentioned constantly throughout the extended Eden narrative (2:9, 17; 3:5, 11) and is the sole object of a prohibition placed by God upon the Man (Gen 2:16-17). On this side of history, we wonder why God chose to plant a tree in or near the garden that would eventually lead to the Man's demise. But in the Eden narrative itself, the tree's placement seems logical. The LORD God planted the tree of the knowledge of good and evil and allowed it to be present in His creation so that the Man would understand both his moral freedom and his spiritual obligation to Yahweh. Much like the children of Israel in the wilderness, the tree of knowledge existed to prove, humble, and try man to see whether he would obey God (Deut 8:2). God's initiatory process taught the Man that he was to be cerebral, practical, and spiritual—the totality of mature masculinity.

We Come to the Garden

We must enter into sacred space alone with God if we will allow ourselves to be initiated by Him. Unlike Adam, we will not be planted in a secret garden and given a primer on early agricultural techniques. Instead, we enter sacred space when we approach the throne of God (or providentially find ourselves there) and seek initiation through prayer and devotion. Sacred space is not limited to a Mesopotamian paradise or a contemporary sanctuary. In fact, it is not so much a physical location as it is a state of mind—a state of being in the presence of God and allowing ourselves to be transformed by His Word. By seeking to connect with God and pursing silence we can enter into His presence.

Once in His presence, the LORD serves as our Initiator and teaches us what He desires of us as men. God communicates with us during initiation through several different mediums. He often makes use of circumstances and situations of life and even employs men whom we may respect. Nevertheless, the primary mode that God uses to communicate with us during the initiatory process is written revelation. Through the Word of God, we come to know Christ (Heb 1:1-2). By coming to know Christ, we learn more of God, for Christ is the "exact imprint of His nature" (Heb 1:3). By growing in our knowledge of both the Father and the Son, we are "conformed to the image of His Son" (Rom 8:29) and initiated into mature masculinity. Bly rightly noted, "When a father and son do spend long hours together, which some fathers and sons still do, we could say that a substance almost like food passes from the older body to the younger." When such time is spent with the true Father, such an exchange is invaluable.

On September 6, 2014, a mob of teens filled a Kroger parking lot in Memphis, Tennessee and beat three people as part of a gang initiation. While some in the group chanted the name of a Memphis-based mob, two Kroger employees were beaten and left unconscious on the sidewalk after the mob was dispersed by security. Within three days, eleven people were arrested and connected to in the incident. All eleven of those arrested were under the age of nineteen. Mark Sauser, the father of one of the victims, attributed the attack to a breakdown of the family. He said, "There's no family structure—kids who've never had a dad. What kind of life is that? Not a single person can replace your dad—not a single person can."

Our society is in desperate need of older men who are willing and capable of assisting boys in their transition to manhood. These mature men take young men apart and serve as copper connectors to God Himself. By modeling biblical masculinity and teaching younger men about passion and productivity for the glory of God, these older men offer an invaluable service to our communities and our culture. Like the first man, Sons of Dust must be initiated in order to fully become what God desires for us to be. During initiation, Yahweh welcomes us into the fullness of manhood by showing us who we truly are. John Eldridge writes of initiation,

> What God sees when he sees you is the real you, the true you, the man he had in mind when he made you… You must ask God what he things of you, and you must stay with the question until you have an answer.

What God sees once a man has been initiated is Christ Jesus alive in him (Gal 2:20), a vessel prepared for great adventure.

5

BECAUSE IT'S THERE

> And God blessed them. And God said to them, "Be fruitful and multiply and fill the earth and subdue it, and have dominion over the fish of the sea and over the birds of the heavens and over every living thing that moves on the earth."
>
> Gen 1:28

There are certain natural wonders that capture the attention and imagination of men. I can remember one of the first writing assignments I was ever given. We had been studying geography in elementary school; hence, I chose to write about Angel Falls, the tallest waterfall in the world. As a child, Angel Falls, a waterfall in Venezuela with a height of over three thousand feet, arrested me. I can remember envisioning what it must have been like to see the Falls for the first time, to see the water plunging thousands of feet before cascading off the rocks below. As an adult, natural formations and wonders still amaze me. Several years ago, I read *Into Thin Air* by Jon Krakauer and marveled at the determination of men like Sir Edmund Hillary, Tenzing Norgay, and George Mallory.

Mallory, one of the early mountaineers who dedicated themselves to summiting the twenty-nine-thousand-foot mountain, is particularly enthralling. Mallory and Andrew Irvine were last seen alive on June 8, 1924, about two thousand feet shy of the top of Everest. Though dressed in warm tweed clothing and equipped with primitive oxygen systems, Mallory and Irvine succumbed to the elements on the side of the mountain and were left dead and unrecovered for seventy-five years. In 1999, a team of mountaineers located Mallory's body and buried him on the side of the mountain. When many think about Mallory's loss of life, they repeat a question that some asked the mountaineer when he was living: "What is the use of climbing Everest?" Here is how George Mallory responded:

> My answer must at once be, "It is of no use." There is not the slightest prospect of any gain whatsoever ... Nothing will come of it. We shall not bring back a single bit of gold or silver, not a gem, nor any coal or iron ... If you cannot understand that there is something in man which responds to the challenge of this mountain and goes out to meet it, that the struggle is the struggle of life itself upward and forever upward, then you won't see why we go. What we get from this adventure is just sheer joy. And joy is, after all, the end of life. We do not live to eat and make money. We eat and make money to be able to live. That is what life means and what life is for.

The truth in Mallory's words haunts and inspires me. Much of what many men do daily is simply for the prospect of financial gain. Very few men actually live. Even fewer men enjoy adventure on a regular basis. Mallory often gave a shorter answer. Why did he climb the mountain? "Because it's there."

Four Rivers

God created man for adventure. Man was made for exploration. After the recording of the creation of the Man and his garden home, the narrator in Gen 2 does something puzzling: he devotes no less than five verses to a description of the rivers in and around the garden in Eden (Gen 2:10-14).

> A river flowed out of Eden to water the garden, and there it divided and became four rivers. The name of the first is the Pishon. It is the one that flowed around the whole land of Havilah, where there is gold. And the gold of that land is good; bdellium and onyx stone are there. The name of the second river is the Gihon. It is the one that flowed around the whole land of Cush. And the name of the third river is the Tigris, which flows east of Assyria. And the fourth river is the Euphrates.
>
> Gen 2:10-14

The text describes one river that flowed out of Eden itself for the purpose of watering the garden that would be inhabited by the Man. This river was later divided—presumably by divine fiat—into four rivers: the Pishon, Gihon, Tigris, and Euphrates. Of these four rivers, we can only be relatively certain about the location of the final two; the Pishon and the Gihon. Though certain clues are provided in the narrative, they cannot be identified definitively and do not necessarily correspond to any waterways that can be located today.

When reading these verses, it is easy to miss the forest for the trees. God is wanting us to grasp more than a secret geographic location. When we read these verses like a Spanish conquistador or Meriweather Lewis, we can begin to comprehend what God is trying to communicate. Gold, bdellium, and onyx are mentioned specifically, as are the lands of Havilah, Cush, and Assyria. The text is filled with adventure, fortune, and exploration. To focus on geography alone is to miss the point. God is introducing the Man to a world ready for charting, exploring, and dominating. God's desire for the first man is summarized early in the book of Genesis: "Be fruitful and multiply and fill the earth and subdue it, and have dominion over the fish of the sea and over the birds of the heavens and over every living thing that moves on the earth" (Gen 1:28). The LORD created a world ready to be subdued, a creation that was prepared for the taking.

About 1,600 years after the creation of man, God gave a similar command to Noah and his sons: "Be fruitful and multiply and fill the earth" (Gen 9:1). The face of the earth may have been entirely altered by the waters of the global flood; nevertheless, the drive for adventure placed by God within the heart of man was not diminished. Later in the biblical record, David, Solomon, and others would be inspired by the same spirit to lead Israel to the height of its prosperity. Paul, the apostle to the Gentiles, was motivated to travel throughout the Mediterranean and preach the Gospel of Christ, often in the face of incredible hardship (2 Cor 11:23-28). Jesus Christ possessed this same adventurous spirit to an infinite degree. Christ left the security of heaven and stepped out of the timelessness of eternity when He was born of the virgin (Gal 4:4). He willingly embarked upon a mission to face temptation (Matt 4:1-11), overcome the world (John 16:33), and sacrificially give Himself as a ransom for sin (Phil 2:5-8).

The Adventurous Spirit

Adam, Noah, David, Jesus, and Paul all modeled an attribute that is indispensable to the masculine spirit—adventure. As John Eldridge states, "Adventure, with all its requisite danger and wildness, is a deeply spiritual longing written into the soul of man." The need for adventure and exploration is so ingrained within man that rejecting it is to risk losing himself. Early in life, we find it easier to connect with our adventurous spirit. We dream of being pilots, astronauts, or archaeologists. We pretend to make new scientific discoveries or conquer lost tribes in some nameless jungle. Somewhere between adolescence and adulthood, we forget that we were made for the domination of the earth. Eldridge notes again:

> The secret longing of your heart, whether it's to build a boat and sail it, to write a symphony and play it, to plant a field and care for it—those are the things you were made to do. That's what you're here for. Explore, build, conquer—you don't have to tell a boy to do those things for the simple reason that it is his purpose.

The gold and ore, the rivers and the lakes that God created in the beginning foreshadow forests, offices, sciences, and fields that are to be subjugated by creative expression and steadfast energy. This masculine quality has always admired in every age. Bly writes, "Men have been loved for their astonishing initiative: embarking on wide oceans, starting a farm in rocky country from scratch, imagining a new business, doing it skillfully, working with beginnings, doing what has never been done."

God has created man to constantly spread the borders of his experience. For Adam, that meant exploring the areas in and around Eden. Noah understood it to mean re-charting a changed earth. Alexander embarked upon world domination. The Founding Fathers pushed the boundaries of democracy. For Einstein and Edison, it implied discovery and invention. Hemingway and Yeats chose to exercise their adventurous natures by means of pen and ink.

The adventurous spirit, though existent in adolescence, must be brought under the control of the overarching rule of the greater masculine spirit. Far from being smoldered, masculinity inflames and promotes the drive of exploration by enabling man to expand himself. As Moore and Gillette notice, "The truth is that the boy in each of us—when he is in his appropriate place in our lives—is the source of playfulness, of pleasure, of fun, of energy, of a kind of open-mindedness, that is ready for adventure and for the future."

The Adventurous Church

This adventurous spirit is employed by God when He directs men to expand the borders of His Kingdom. Having ascended back to the Father, Jesus entrusted the expansion of His church to thirteen men who would carry the Gospel to the entire world (Matt 28:18-20; Col 1:23). By the close of the first century, the church had spread throughout Asia Minor, Greece, Rome, and northern Africa. Undoubtedly, the news of Jesus had spread even further than the places revealed in the New Testament, having been conveyed by those who heard the preaching of the disciples of Christ. The entire early church was consumed with the proclamation and spread of the Gospel; the growth of the church was driven by this adventurous spirit.

In 2014, *Time* chose an overlooked segment of the world population as their "Person of the Year." The honor was awarded to a group of people the publication called "The Ebola Fighters." One of these individuals, Dr. Kent Brantly, received national attention when he contracted the communicable disease and had to be transferred from Liberia to Atlanta for treatment. Brantly, a Christian, had personally seen only one person survive an Ebola infection when he was diagnosed. After receiving treatment, he recovered. A month later, the doctor remarked that he would like to return to western Africa to help treat others if the Lord was willing. What was it that allowed Kent Brantly to put himself in harm's way in order to help others? One characteristic—one among many others—is the same adventurous nature that God instilled within the first man.

Sons of Dust, men who are dedicated to Christ and His church, are still valued for their adventurous character and, sometimes, playful nature. Instead of wondering, "Why?" biblical men ask, "Why not?" They undertake great feats for the glory of God and the purpose of taking the Gospel to all the world.

6

THE WARRIOR WITHIN

> Saul has struck down his thousands, and David his ten thousands.
>
> 1 Sam 18:7

There are certain shades of masculinity—even biblical manliness—from which we shy away. Generally, the 21st-century populace is uneasy when discussing male assertiveness and the more conflict-focused characteristics associated with men. Even Christianity chooses to overlook the fierce side of the traditional man and has idolized soft, neutered men in the past. This rejection of the fighting spirit has left modern men confused, seeking a safe, socially-acceptable outlet for something God has placed within them. Mixed martial arts, blood-and-gore films, and senseless violence have been entirely unable to fill this void in the masculine soul and have only contributed to the diluted machoism characterized on prime-time sitcoms.

As John Eldridge states, "Aggression is part of the masculine design; we are hardwired for it. If we believe that man is made in the image of God, then we would do well to remember that 'the LORD is a warrior; the Lord is his name,' (Ex. 15:3)." God, in His infinite wisdom and in accordance with His divine purpose, has created man to be fierce—to play the part of the warrior, the defender, and the conqueror. The desire to share in the battle is so engrained within every man that to neutralize it is steal a valuable piece of his God-given masculinity. When society, family, or even the church robs a man of his warrior spirit, they attack his strength "one vertebra at a time, until in the end he has no spine at all," as says Eldridge. This aggressive nature is so engrained in every man that it is universal. Moore and Gillette write,

> The Warrior energy ... no matter what else it may be, is indeed universally present in us men and in the civilizations we create, defend, and extend. It is a vital ingredient in our world-building and plays an important role in extending the benefits of the highest human virtues and cultural achievements to all of humanity.

God instilled this spirit within the Man and gave it His blessing. After having created the Man and constructing for him a home, Moses records, "The LORD God took the man and put him in the garden of Eden to work it and keep it" (Gen 2:15).

God placed the Man in the field of battle—the garden in Eden—and gave him a specific mission. First, the Man was told to "work" the garden itself. Our progenitor was given the divine command to till the ground, planting and cultivating the very earth from which he had been derived (Gen 2:5). As a tiller, the Man would plan, plant, and procure all that the earth could or would offer. He would employ his intelligence, his creativity, and his own desires in service to his God. Second, God commanded the Man to "keep" his garden home. While such terminology is often used to refer to observing the commands of God (Gen 17:9; Lev 18:5; Num 3:7-8), the word is also used for protecting, defending, and maintaining something or someone else (Gen 4:9; 30:31). Essentially, the Man was told to cultivate the garden and to protect and defend it by force, if need be. The Man was told to be aggressive, to conquer and defend his new habitat. Thus, God provides the first glimpse of the warrior spirit that He instilled within man—a spirit of creative expression and controlled aggression.

This same energy has been harnessed by righteous men throughout history. Abraham fought against the coalition of kings (Gen 14). Moses and Joshua both led Israel in battle (Exo 17). The judges and the early kings were praised for their prowess in battle. Some of the most honored men in the Old Testament were warriors. Lest we be deceived into thinking that the warrior's sword was laid to rest with the birth of Christ, we need to be reminded that even the Son of God was aggressive and warlike when dealing with the money grubbers of His day (John 2:15). Likewise, the apostles of Christ knew how to give a scathing rebuke or deliver an apostolic threat of force (Acts 5:1-11; 8:20-23; 1 Cor 4:21). Soldier or military imagery is used repeatedly in the New Testament (Phil 2:25; 2 Tim 2:3-4; Eph 6:10-18).

Bly recognized that "most people, men or women, do not know what genuine outward or inward warriors would look like, or feel like." This lack of the warrior spirit has led to the detriment, not the betterment, of society as a whole. In Gen 2, God shows us what a warrior looks like. Sons of Dust are warriors, but a warrior without a King is a ronin—a wandering samurai with no lord. The Man in our narrative has a King, Yahweh God. He also is instructed in strategy and creativity, as well as force and ferocity.

Our General

Radical feminists and an uninformed populace have learned to fear the warrior aspect of masculinity. They equate aggression with wanton war, destruction, and erratic violence. But according to Eldridge,

> You cannot teach a boy to use his strength by stripping him of it ... It may look moral, it may look like turning the other cheek, but it is merely weakness. You cannot turn a cheek you do not have. Our churches are full of such men.

Much of our trepidation about the aggressive masculine nature resolves itself when each man is in service to a king. "A man is a dangerous thing," writes Eldridge. "So is a scalpel. It can wound or it can save your life. You don't make it safe by making it dull; you put it in the hands of someone who knows what he's doing."

The original man was placed into the hands of the LORD. The Man was taken by God and placed in the garden, a place where Yahweh desired for him to be. The Man was debriefed—given specific directions, challenges, and objectives. God told him where to go, what to do, and how to accomplish his mission. While the details and particulars were left up to his own cunning, God made sure that ample direction was given to His warrior to make the mission successful. As such, God operated as the general; the Man was the foot soldier. Yahweh truly was the Lord. Man was the samurai.

Some men reject the oversight and directing governance of God. William Ernest Henley was one such man. In his poem *Invictus*, he writes,

> It matters not how strait the gate,
>   How charged with punishments the scroll,
> I am the master of my fate,
> I am the captain of my soul.

This spirit of independence and autonomy leads to a perversion of the warrior spirit that degenerates, as Bly writes, into "domination, treating people as if they were objects, demanding land or empire, holding on to the Cold War—the whole model of machismo." King Saul, Alexander the Great, and Adolf Hitler all operated as Shadow Warriors, living as a law unto themselves and wreaking havoc on the world around them. True warriors serve as a welcome anthesis to this destruction and rage.

When man as a warrior is subservient to a transcendent cause, he is able to capitalize on the aggressive nature that God has placed within him. Eldridge noticed that God has, in an incredible act of grace, welcomed man as his apprentice and fellow warrior.

> A man must have a battle to fight, a great mission to his life that involves and yet transcends even home and family. He must have a cause to which he is devoted in unto death … You do. That is why God created you—to be his intimate ally, to join him in the Great Battle.

God is able to take the warrior spirit that He Himself has placed within man and cultivate, nurture, and develop it in a healthy way for His glory. Courage, fortitude, self-control, and all spiritual characteristics associated with the warrior are wholly developed in the presence of God (Deut 31:6; Gal 5:22-23). God, as the General, brings out the best in His men. As Bly remarked, when a warrior is connected with God and given a transcendent cause, "he does well, and his body becomes a hardworking servant, which he requires to endure cold, heat, pain, wounds, scarring, hunger, lack of sleep, hardship of all kinds." It is possible for a warrior, when necessary, to become a near ascetic for the cause. Interestingly, Moore and Gillette said that the warrior

> lives a life exactly the opposite of most human lives. He lives not to gratify his personal needs and wishes or his physical appetites but to hone himself into an efficient spiritual machine, trained to bear the unbearable in the service of the transpersonal goal.

Without Christ, his transcendent cause, Paul would have been unable to endure all the hardships he faced during his ministry (2 Cor 11:23-28). While in service under Christ, the apostle Paul encountered abasement and abuse; he went hungry and suffered from want. But Christ strengthened him (Phil 4:11-13). Everything about his life was motivated by submissive self-control (1 Cor 9:27); when Paul submitted as a soldier to Christ Jesus, he was able to unlock his potential and maximize his effectiveness as a soldier. Living in connection with Christ helped to channel the aggressiveness toward evangelization and edification of the body of Christ, even if it meant direct confrontation on occasion (Gal 2:11-14).

The fierce, aggressive, and courageous spirit nestled within the breast of every man is placed there by God and intended to be used in service unto Him. When we are channelling this attribute of biblical manliness correctly, "we will be," according to Moore and Gillette, "energetic, decisive, courageous, enduring, persevering, and loyal to some greater good beyond our own personal gain."

To Protect and Serve

In 1955, Officer Joseph Dorobek entered a contest held by BEAT magazine to create a new motto for the Los Angeles Police Academy. His motto—the winning entry—was simple: "To Protect and to Serve." The motto was quickly adopted by the academy and later became ubiquitous in the department as a whole when it was placed beside the City Seal on patrol cars. "To Protect and to Serve," while originally only the motto for the Los Angeles Police Department, has been used by law enforcement officers throughout the United States.

Interestingly enough, the Man was placed in the garden in Eden "to protect and to serve." Moses, the inspired narrator, reveals that God intended for man to serve by working the ground and to protect by keeping or defending his garden home. These traditional masculine values—service and protection—are deeply engrained within the heart of every man.

The call for man to work the ground, to cultivate the earth, and develop resources that are useful is directly linked to the role of service. On the surface, his obedience to God's direct command

and charge illustrates that the Man was willingly serving the Lord. However, the service alluded to goes even deeper than that. The Man had just witnessed God creating vegetation from the ground, planting a garden, and filling it with all types of plant-life. Yahweh didn't simply cultivate those plants that were good for food; instead, visually stimulating and beautiful herbage was found in His cultivated corner of Eden (Gen 2:8-9). What the Lord did by miraculous cultivation was intended for man's natural replication. It would take nothing less than a warrior to meet the challenges presented in the garden and overcome them. The Man would need to employ creativity, cunningness, and intelligence to accomplish his mission.

The warrior within each of us involves more than physical confrontation and destruction. Real soldiers must possess a certain prowess, an eye that has been trained to evaluate the situation and choose a course of action that may not be entirely apparent to those who are untrained. Gillette and Moore write,

> The warrior is always alert. He is always awake. He is never sleeping through life. He knows how to focus his mind and his body. He is what the samurai called "mindful." He is a "hunter" in the Native American tradition...he is a strategist and a tactician. He can evaluate his circumstances accurately and then adapt himself to the "situation on the ground," as we say.

David knew how to creatively adapt to the situation confronting him (1 Sam 21:10-15). Whether of his own imagination or by divine command, Gideon used trumpets, lamps, and pots to lead three hundred men to victory (Judg 7:16-22). Joab climbed up a water shaft to conquer the inhabitants of Jebus (2 Sam 5:6-8; 1 Chr 11:6). Eldridge states, "A warrior is cunning. He knows when to fight and when to run; he can sense a trap and never charges blindly ahead; he knows what weapons to carry and how to use them." The warrior spirit within modern men helps them not only in combat, but also as they navigate the tumultuous waters of personal relations, church work, and family obligations. It aids us in using all we have to develop all that we can. The aggressive masculine nature motivates men to "Be All You Can Be."

A keen eye without decisive action never wins battles, hence God instructed the man not only to serve in the garden but to protect it as well. This protection included keeping it free from intruders—whoever that might have been—and defending it at all costs. The Man was to protect himself, his home, and his wife who was yet to be created. While Cain rejected this aspect of his being and descended into the shadows (Gen 4:9), the first man was created to be the Lord's warrior.

Conflict and even destruction can be a healthy part of being a warrior, so long as the conflict is resolved and the destruction is used to make way for something positive and constructive. Much of Jesus's public teaching involved head-to-head conflict with the religious teachers of His day. His "You have heard that it was said," (Matt 5:21, 27, 33, 38, 43) and His "Woe to you, scribes and Pharisees, hypocrites," (Matt 23:13, 23, 25, 27, 29) highlight two occasions wherein the Lord channeled the aggressive part of His nature. His assault had a purpose—the removal of the veil of deception from the face of the Jewish population.

Unfortunately, both fierce offense and tenacious defense for the cause of Christ have given way to a silent passivity among modern men. Instead of adopting a healthy model of conflict resolution—one used with great success by the early church (Acts 15:1-21)—the modern church has avoided debate and disagreement and, in doing so, has rejected a great catalyst for spiritual growth. Bly noticed this loss in the secular realm when he wrote, "The disappearance of fierce debates is a loss...Both science and literature advance by means of ritual battles between generations."

The LORD God expected for the Man to be fierce enough to fight when the need arose. By the same token, we, as Sons of Dust, are expected to rise to the occasion. The fate of the church and our own homes hangs in the balance. "The fading of the warrior contributes to the collapse of civilized society," wrote Bly. "A man who cannot defend his own space cannot defend women and children."

Passive Aggressive

More needs to be said about the aggressive nature of the warrior of God, particularly as touching passivity. Too many Christian men are overly passive. The blessing of Christ upon the meek (Matt 5:5) and Paul's command to be gentle (2 Tim 2:24) have been wrested and contorted into shackles that bind too many good men. While Jesus instructed men to "turn the other cheek" (Matt 5:39), He never intended for men to bat their eye at sin, degradation, and corruption. The warrior within every man was placed there to promote action. Theodore Roosevelt said, "One prime reason for abhorring cowards is because every good boy should have it in him to thrash the objectionable boy as the need arise." Sometimes, biblical men need to be the ones who are doing the thrashing, but more often than we'd like to admit, we are comfortable sitting on the sidelines.

Passivity has long been the thorn in the side of our fighting spirit. Even the Man gave into passivity when the serpent beguiled his wife. Were he upholding the LORD's command to protect the garden, the Man would have driven the serpent from his paradise. Eldridge wrote, "Our first father—the first real man—gave in to paralysis...We won't risk, we won't fight, and we won't rescue Eve. We truly are a chip off the old block." The passive man waits for someone else to take initiative—whether that "someone" be his wife, his children, or another generation of God-fearing men. He procrastinates, avoids engagement, and operates reactively instead of proactively. He is never content, but never courageous enough to make a change. Unlike Paul, he is not willing to strain for what lies ahead or "press on toward the goal," (Phil 3:13-14). There are too many positive, active commands in the New Testament for men of God to be passive and reactive. Take 1 Thess. 5:12-22 for an example: respect, esteem, and be at peace; admonish, encourage, help, and be patient; seek to do good to one another and to everyone; rejoice, pray, and give thanks; test everything and hold fast. The warrior doesn't hesitate. He remains ready, prepared for whatever action he may be called on to undertake for the glory of his Master.

Writing of the warrior, Moore and Gillette said,

> Aggressiveness is a stance toward life that rouses, energizes, and motivates. It pushes us to take the offensive and to move out of a defensive or "holding" position about life's tasks and problems. The samurai

advice was always to "leap" into battle with the full potential of ki, or "vital energy," at your disposal. The Japanese warrior tradition claimed that there is only one position in which to face the battle of life: frontally. And it also proclaimed that there was only one direction: forward.

God has never intended for his men to be passive and neutral. biblical men are warriors capable of spiritually defending themselves, their homes, and their churches. This essential characteristic is lacking in many churches and must be recaptured if we are to preserve Biblical manliness. The first man was endowed with a fighters spirit. So are we. Jesus said, "The kingdom of heaven has suffered violence, and the violent take it by force" (Matt 11:12). If we are going to possess biblical manliness, then we must have the courage, strength, fortitude, and initiative to defend it.

7

GIVE ME LIBERTY

> The Spirit of the Lord GOD is upon me, because the LORD has anointed me to bring good news to the poor; he has sent me to bind up the brokenhearted, to proclaim liberty to the captives, and the opening of the prison to those who are bound.
>
> Isa 61:1

Having placed the Man in the midst of the perfect paradise in Eden, God gave him a set of direct commands. The language of Gen 2:16-17 is incredibly direct; Yahweh did not want to be misunderstood. The narrator records that the LORD God *commanded* the Man. The Creator did not make a divine suggestion or give a take-it-or-leave-it comment. His words were piercing and pointed directly at the center of man's being.

> And the LORD God commanded the man saying, "You may surely eat of every tree of the garden, but of the tree of the knowledge of good and evil you shall not eat, for in the day that you eat of it you shall surely die.
>
> Gen 2:16-17

God had already dealt with several aspects of the Man's being through a series of divinely arranged acts. The Man knew that he was a farmer created to till the ground and care for the garden in Eden. He was aware that his task also included protecting his home, serving Yahweh as a warrior with a mission from the Almighty. God had given the man a brief, yet concentrated, initiation through which the Man learned that he was more than flesh and bones. Now, by directing attention to the trees in the garden, Yahweh seeks to instill within the Man that he is a spiritual being, a person capable of great accomplishments or horrible ruin.

Herein lies one of the greatest problems with the majority of modern men. It's easy for us to embrace exploration, adventure, and even a warrior-like spirit, yet still maintain something similar to the socially accepted form of modern masculinity. However, when we acknowledge that we are spiritual beings with obligations to a God Whom we have never seen and destined for an eternal home which we have never visited, we separate ourselves from the current classification of manliness and support a banner only held aloft by radicals and fringe-men.

Nevertheless, the foundation of biblical masculinity stands firm. It is impossible to possess biblical masculinity without an understanding of the Bible; it is impossible to be one of God's men without experiencing the reality of a life connected with God. This understanding, this grasping of truth not entirely discernible without a divine revelation from God, is imperative in the life of a man. Men will find something to worship—money, power, ego, football. But nothing is capable of satisfying the spiritual longing of a man's heart other than God. During his sermon on Mars Hill,

Paul spoke to a group of Athenians who were spiritual but had yet to find true connection with God. Their misunderstanding—their ignorance—kept them from developing to their full potential (Acts 17:30). Knowledge is directly connected with Christian growth and development (2 Pet 1:2-6).

The Man received a knowledge from God in the garden in Eden. The LORD showed the Man that a balance of permission and prohibition, coupled with a dedication to faithfulness, was necessary for man to fulfill his purpose.

Permission

The first half of God's command to the Man is one of license—"You may surely eat of every tree of the garden" (Gen 2:16). Just in case the newly created Man had any qualms about partaking of the bountiful plants God had produced, the LORD grants him permission. The Man had the ability to consider his own desires, recognize that God had given him liberty, and choose whatever sustenance he liked. We can imagine that each indulgence would warrant a certain measure of praise. Every nibble was granted by the permission given by an omni-benevolent God. Through this exercise of selection, ingestion, and adoration, we can see how a deep appreciation and respect for the Man's Creator would be fostered.

Man, as a being, needs liberty. He needs the ability to choose, select, and exercise his own will. Part of man's partnership with God stems from the mutual interaction of the will of man with the will of God. Bly wrote,

> To receive initiation truly means to expand sideways into the glory of oaks, mountains, glaciers, horses, lions, grasses, waterfalls, deer. We need wilderness and extravagance. Whatever shuts a human being away from the waterfall and the tiger will kill him.

This sense of liberty and license is paramount in the Bible, especially in the New Testament. An essential aspect of the Gospel of Christ is liberty itself. Christ came preaching that those who were captive—both to sin and the restrictive nature of the perversion of the Law—would be set free (Isa 61:1; Luke 4:18). The liberating quality of the Gospel is so essential to its nature that the New Testament itself is called "the law of liberty," (Jas 1:25). Where the Spirit of the Lord is, there is liberty (2 Cor 3:17); all the children of God are free (Rom 8:21). The free and freeing nature of the Law of Christ is to be defended, respected, and enjoyed (Gal 5:1).

We do Christianity a great disservice when we seek to simplify the Gospel by boiling it down to a list of do's and don't's. In his notable book on manliness, John Eldridge states,

> When all is said and done, I think most men in the church believe that God put them on the earth to be a good boy…That's what we hold up as models of Christian maturity: Really Nice Guys. We don't smoke, drink, or swear; that's what makes us men.

Eldridge gets even more pointed later in his book.

> What does the church bring a man into? What does it call him out to be? Moral. That is pitifully insufficient.

> Morality is a good thing, but morality is never the point.

He's right. "Morality is never the point." There's a great deal more to biblical manliness than morality. A checklists of moral obligations is a far cry from true godliness and, by extension, true masculinity. A young man came to Jesus on one occasion. "Good teacher," he said, "what must I do to inherit eternal life?" After the Lord's command to keep the commandments, the young man informed the Lord that he was not guilty of murder, adultery, theft, deceit, or disobedience. If morality in and of itself was enough, Christ would have sent the rich young man merrily on his way, but He didn't. Jesus told him to go home, sell his possessions, give his money to the poor, and then to come back and follow Him. The lad went away sorrowing because he had a lot of stuff (Mark 10:17-22). Notice that Christ didn't condemn him for his morality; nevertheless, Jesus did communicate that his life was lacking something. What was missing? Passionate action. "Go…sell…give…come…follow"—all of these words describe the actions and choices ripe for the picking.

Prohibition

Now that we have sufficiently established that Biblical manliness is more than simply moral living, we need to return to the narrative of Gen 2. Lest we think that commandment keeping is completely against the definition of masculinity, Yahweh attaches a prohibition to his command as He delivers it to the Man. After giving man liberty, the LORD God said, "But of the tree of the knowledge of good and evil you shall not eat, for in the day that you eat of it you shall surely die" (Gen 2:17). God's command is pretty simple; the Man could eat anything in the garden except for the fruit from the tree of the knowledge of good and evil. This tree—this one tree—was entirely off limits. Our prototype could have anything but this fruit.

What was it about the tree of the knowledge of good and evil that was so different? The tree of knowledge was one of two special trees planted by God Himself; the tree of life was the other. While the tree of life is mentioned and then only brought up again at the end of the Eden narrative (Gen 3:22-24), the tree of knowledge is central to the story. We know that this tree was planted in the midst of the garden in Eden (Gen 3:3), forbidden (Gen 2:17), known by both the Man and his woman (Gen 3:3), was good for food, a delight to the eyes, and desirable to make one wise (Gen 3:6). The text also states that through the eating of this fruit, the Edenic couple became conscious of their nakedness and felt shame (Gen 3:7, 10). Other than those things which are revealed, not much more can be known. We are left with a lot of unanswered questions.

We can know one thing for certain. The tree of the knowledge of good and evil served as a test or trial for the Man. Just like God tried the Israelites in the wilderness (Deut 8:2) and allowed remnants of the heathen nations to serve as a test for the settlers of Canaan (Judg 2:21-22), Yahweh used the tree of knowledge to try the Man, to see whether he would choose to obey God or not. "Foul!" some cry, "Since God knew that Adam would sin, why did He plant the tree of knowledge in the first place?" He did so to give the Man liberty, something that God—in His divine wisdom—created man to need. In giving man this limited freedom, God also granted him the ability to choose wrong. That's where the prohibitive nature of God's command is brought into focus.

God graciously informed the Man of the harmful nature of the tree of knowledge. The act of partaking of its fruit would cause death. The wordage of God's prohibition carries with it all the regality and severity of a royal decree or proclamation (Gen 20:7; 1 Sam 14:39; Ezek 33:8, 14). The violation of God's covenant would bring about death. Undoubtedly, God intended for the seriousness of this prohibition to be felt by His creation. Why did God forbid man from eating of the tree? Love. God wanted what was best for the Man—an ongoing relationship with his Creator only possible through holiness, faithfulness, and love.

Why would God impose restrictions upon His own children? Love. A biblical man rejoices in the liberty he has in Christ but respects the prohibitions God has placed on certain practices as well. Some modern "men" flaunt their supposed Christian liberty while scorning the prohibitions delivered by Christ through His Gospel. They never recognize that God has marked certain things as "Off Limits" for their benefit (Gal 5:19-21). When we choose to reject the commands of God and exercise our own moral autonomy, we are guilty of the same sin our forefather committed. We reject His way and choose to declare our independence.

Patrick Henry is most often cited for having said, "Give me liberty or give me death!" The first Man was given liberty, but chose death instead. In Christ, all men are given liberty, but sadly, many still choose death. We've been given freedom from death, sin, and hell; however, our allegiance is not to our self to fulfill our own fleshly lusts (Eph 2:3). Instead, we have been bought by God (1 Cor 6:20) and owe our life to God.

Revelation

Both permission and prohibition were made known to the Man by the revelation of God. Such was an act of God's grace. I suppose the LORD could have planted the tree of knowledge in the midst of the garden and provided no warning whatsoever; however, God showed Himself to be a loving and just Father by giving ample warning for the dangers of the forbidden fruit. Biblical masculinity is intricately connected with biblical revelation. It is impossible to have the former without the later. It is essential for the Sons of Dust to be men of the Book if they desire to live up to their potential.

Unfortunately, men generally spurn learning, especially learning that is connected with the Bible. Most men see little value in any type of Bible study, for if we did see its merit, we would not have to be coerced into reading our Bible daily. Eldridge puts it this way:

> Most men have a hard time sustaining any sort of devotional life because it has no vital connection to recovering and protecting their strength; it feels about as important as flossing. But if you saw your life as a great battle and you knew you needed time with God for your very survival, you would do it.

If we understood that uncovering the truths of the Bible were essential to unlocking the deepest riches of our masculinity, then we would be serious students. The written word of God is vital to the life of a man. God's word was originally spoken to Adam, but now we receive the word through the written word (Heb 1:1-3). In the pages of the Bible, we find all that we need to live a full and fulfilling life (2 Pet 1:3; 2 Tim 3:16-17). Liberty itself is connected with an understanding of the precepts of God—both positive and prohibitive (Psa 119:45).

There is a reason why God chooses the leaders of the church from a collection of men who are not novices (1 Tim 3:6); He intends for Christian men to be gentleman scholars. Fathers are to rear their children to know the Lord (Eph 6:4); husbands are to live with their wives after knowledge (1 Pet 3:7). This understanding gives biblical men an enormous amount of power—power to connect themselves, their families, and others with God Himself. Men must not be afraid or ashamed Bible study, for through regular exploration into the Word we are brought closer to God and develop a deeper love and appreciation for the secret things that belong to Him alone (Deut 29:29).

Abundant Lives

God knew the Man needed the freedom to adequately express himself and revel in the paradise God had planted for him. His divine permission granted the Man the ability to explore and enjoy the fruits of the garden. We have the same permission as modern men. God has given us the liberty to live full lives and develop into our fullest potential (John 10:10). However, God's love is more than license. Sometimes Yahweh prohibits out of love as well.

The Bible is more than a book recording the creation and history of man from a divine perspective. It is a vast treasure trove of knowledge capable of leading men to eternal life found only in Christ. Man as a spiritual being needs sustenance—the spiritual food that only Christ can provide (John 6:53). His Words are spirit and life (John 6:63). Without the Word of God, a man will starve like a vagabond in the desert. We need the Word of God to live.

8

THE KING OF THE JUNGLE

> The heavens are the LORD's heavens, but the earth he has given to the children of man.
>
> Ps 115:16

There are certain aspects concerning man's nature from which American society and culture have thoroughly insulated us. One such aspect is the regal, kingly part of man's soul—the aspect of manliness that rules over his own domain and brings peace and blessing to those under his oversight. Members of generations past the world over were able to direct their own attention to thrones, castles, and palaces and recall the value of a king, especially a benevolent one. There are no castles in the New World. The Biltmore Estate is the closest we come. To the ancients, the king was directly tied to God. The royal reigned by divine right; the blessing of God rested upon him. The royal king would bestow blessing and confer order upon those in his care, channeling the omni-benevolent nature of his own King. The kings from ancient fairy tales, the majestic monarchs of the Middle Ages, and even Pharaohs of Ancient Egypt were the embodiment of the kingly nature of man in the eyes of their own people. Lincoln, Washington, and Churchill made their kingly presence felt to a certain degree.

The Bible offers several examples of good kings—David, Melchizedek, Josiah, and Jesus to name a few. Each of these men had a marvelous impact upon their people for good. The blessings they brought upon the people was a result of their connection with God. Every good king is intimately connected to the best King. The first king mentioned in the Bible is often overlooked. We know him as "the Man" or "Adam."

The LORD, having created all things and constructed a perfect paradise for man's habitation, had partially initiated the Man into proper manhood. The Man was familiar with his purpose and God's plan. He was debriefed concerning the world intended for his domination, the ground present for his tillage, and the garden he was told to protect. Through revelation, Yahweh made known to the Man the spiritual aspect of his being and labeled a certain tree—the tree of knowledge—as forbidden fruit. Now that the Man had life and liberty, God desired to instill within him the regal heart of a king. The way God chose to reveal this heart to the Man—the same way He determined to unveil it to us in the narrative—is linked with man's responsibility to the earth itself.

> Now out of the ground the LORD God had formed every beast of the field and every bird of the heavens and brought them to the man to see what he would call them. And whatever the man called every living creature, that was its name. The man gave names to all livestock and to the birds of the heavens and to every beast of the field.
>
> Gen 2:19-20

God brought all the animals to the Man and watched as the beasts and birds received their names. Whatever the Man chose to call the animals, that was its name. This act—the Man's first independent action—illustrates the character and duty of the king within every man. Notice that God was not passive; Yahweh did not simply allow the Man to assume his royal responsibility in his own time. Instead, God thrust His Man into kingly action by parading the animals before him. Many men seek to avoid this part of their manhood. They welcome their ferocity, wildness, and even their spirituality, but refuse to accept the responsibilities connected with being a king. God determines when a man is ready to reign, and when the man is ready, God places him in control of a domain.

Naming the Animals

I imagine this scene in the narrative could have been rather comedic. If the narrator were recording the proceedings simply for my benefit, then it would not have been out of place for him to give a few of the names that the Man bestowed upon the animals. However, God chose only to reveal the action of the man. He has left the details of his action hidden. In so doing, Yahweh has drawn attention to what is taking place—the first royal decree given by a newly crowned king.

When God determined to create mankind, He said, "Let us make man in Our image, after Our likeness. And let them have dominion over the fish of the sea and over the birds of the heavens and over the livestock and over all the earth and over every creeping thing that creeps on the earth" (Gen 1:26). Man was created in the image of God, but what does that even mean? Being created in the image of God certainly included the spiritual aspect of man. God endowed the Man—and eventually all men—with an eternal soul. Thus man is a soulful creature similar to God, for God is a spiritual Being (John 4:24). However, being image-bearers of God involves more than possessing a soul. The LORD connected bearing His image with possessing dominion over the creatures of the earth. While God would communicate and associate with the Man directly, his interaction with the rest of creation would be different following the ceasing of His first week of work.

After the Creation Week, God chose to interact with the earth through the agency of man (Ps 115:16). The Man would serve as the ruler, king, and lord of the earth. As the Man reigned righteously through cultivating flora and dominating fauna, he would serve as a mirror that reflected the glory, majesty, and authority of God upon the rest of creation. The LORD commanded such when He said to the Man, "Be fruitful and multiply and fill the earth and subdue it, and have dominion over the fish of the sea and over the birds of the heavens and over every living thing that moves on the earth" (Gen 1:28). So long as the Man correctly exercised the authority vested in him, he reflected the image of God upon the rest of creation. Everything touched by his hand was brought under the authority of God Himself. In Iron John, Bly rightly notes that "the...king is a part of a three-tiered world, and he derives his energy and authority from his ability to be transparent or receptive to the King above."

The Man first embodied the image of God when he bestowed names upon the animals. The text says he called them and gave names to all of them. The act of naming something or someone illustrates dominion. We bestow names upon our pets, our possessions, and even our children. Architects name buildings. Authors title books. We name the things that are under our control. Every name that the Man attached to any beast stuck—"whatever the man called every living creature, that was its name." Each name carried with it the weight of a king, for the Man was the first of God's chosen kings.

The psalmist captured a beautiful portrait of the Man's kingly role when he wrote:

> Yet you have made him a little lower than the heavenly beings and crowned him with glory and honor. You have given him dominion over the works of your hands; you have put all things under his feet, all sheep and oxen, and also the beasts of the field, the birds of the heavens, and the fish of the sea, whatever passes along the paths of the seas.
>
> Ps 8:5-8

All of creation was under the Man's control. That does not mean it was isolated from the intervention of God, for God would intervene momentarily to create the Woman; however, God intended for all of creation to be subject to man, and for the Man to bear Yahweh's name upon the rest of the creation.

Your Domain

The Man was given a specific, but very broad, domain. All of creation was placed under his care. All the animals and plants that had been created by God were to be for his subjugation. More specifically, the first of our kind was given a walled paradise, a garden in Eden, for his realm. The Man would soon be given a wife, thereby granting him yet another territory—a family. Thus, the Man was given a three-fold kingdom: his home, his community, and the world.

As Sons of Dust, God intends for us to exercise dominion over our own domains. Each man—or each male, for that matter—is given a territory to rule. Early in life, our territory may encompass our own bunks, or perhaps our own room. Later, our dominion extends to an automobile, apartment, or dorm room. Office space and job requirements lead to a larger kingdom. Eventually, our solo is transformed to a duo through marriage, and we are given greater responsibilities connected with a larger realm. In whatever season we find ourselves, every man has a kingdom over which God has made him king. In order for us to reign worthily, the LORD intends for us to recognize the extent of our dominion and exercise our authority responsibly and constructively.

Take the life of David as an example. When we are first introduced to David, he is a shepherd who tends to his father's sheep (1 Sam 16:11). His kingdom is a kingdom of wool-covered grass eaters, but he has the heart of a king (1 Sam 16:7). After his victory over Goliath (1 Sam 17), David's sphere of influence extends. Saul placed a thousand men under his control (1 Sam 18:13). Next, David took on the role of husband by his marriage to Michal, Saul's daughter (1 Sam 18:27). David was anointed as king in Hebron after the death of Saul (2 Sam 2:3-4), but his kingdom was limited to the tribe of Judah (2 Sam 2:11). After the assassination of Ishbosheth, David was made king over the whole land of Israel for thirty-three years (2 Sam 5:3-5). Thus, David's kingship began with a flock of sheep and ended with a stretch of territory from Dan to Beersheba.

The circles of our influence and authority often extend in similar ways. Those who have been faithful over smaller territories will be given huge tracts of land—in time of course (Matt 25:21). We first rule ourselves, then our possessions; we have dominion over our families, and then our churches and communities. God intends for each of us to faithfully discharge our royal duties over whatever kingdom He has entrusted to us.

Order, Bless, and Serve

What are the duties and responsibilities of a king? In their book *King, Warrior, Magician, Lover*, Moore and Gillette mention two kingly functions specifically. A king provides both *order* and *blessing*. The first of these roles—the role of order and organizer—provides stability and security for those under the king's control. The second—the conference of blessing—bestows affirmation and worth to others. In both instances, the king functions not for his own benefit, but for the benefit of others. True, as Moore and Gillette put it, "We can be Little Hitlers, but we're going to destroy our country in the process." We can personally enjoy the fruits of our labors by indulging ourselves in our own delights. However, such a corruption of power is not contained in the original design of God. Bly writes,

> The Greeks understood and praised a positive male energy that has accepted authority. They called it Zeus energy, which encompasses intelligence, robust health, compassionate decisiveness, good will, generous leadership. Zeus energy is male authority accepted for the sake of the community.

The Man in the Genesis narrative is actively ordering the animal kingdom. It is doubtful that he took the time to divide all of creation according to their genus, family, order, or class; however, the Man does exhibit rationality, creativity, and sovereignty by applying distinct names to each animal. When a true king is seated upon his throne, he brings order to chaos and synchronizes his entire kingdom. Though synchronization in the home, the church, and the office will be different, we—when we function as kings—will bring order and stability to each. We will exercise the wisdom of Solomon and provide a platform for those under our care to thrive. Families, churches, and organizations that lack a king—or are ruled by tyrants—will descend into dysfunction.

The second role of a king is to provide blessing. Though not described in the text of Gen 2, this function of kings is seen throughout history and down to the present. Bly says, "Everyone wants to be with 'the King.'" Why? Because we all want to be blessed. The patriarchs of the Old Testament often bestowed blessings upon their children. Moses, David, Solomon, and other great leaders interceded with the Lord for the benefit of the nation of Israel. Jesus blessed those around Him by miraculously healing and feeding them. Now Christ sits at the right had of God and provides all spiritual blessings (Eph 1:3). Moore and Gillette write,

> The King archetype in its fullness possesses the qualities of order, of reasonable and rational patterning, of integration and integrity in the masculine psyche. It stabilizes chaotic emotion and out-of-control behaviors. It gives stability and centeredness. It brings calm. And in its "fertilizing" and centeredness, it mediates vitality, life-force, and joy. It brings

maintenance and balance. It defends our own sense of inner order, our own integrity of being and of purpose, our own central calmness about who we are, and our essential unassailability and certainty in our masculine identity. It looks upon the world with a firm but kindly eye. It sees others in all their weakness and in all their talent and worth. It honors them and promotes them. It guides them and nurtures them toward their own fullness of being. It is not envious, because it is secure, as the King, in its own worth. It rewards and encourages creativity in us and in others.

When Jesus spoke of the future leaders in His kingdom, He revealed that they would not necessarily be those who were mighty, charismatic, or noteworthy. Those who would be kings with Christ were those who were willing to serve (Matt 23:11). We are to esteem others as better than ourselves (Phil 2:3) and to serve one another in love (Gal 5:13). If Christ our King came to serve, certainly we—as kings for Christ—are destined for service as well. None should imagine that their regality is inherited by right of birth alone. For a man, the throne is not bought, stolen, or won. It is earned and maintained through service.

Lost in Adam, Gained in Christ

Unfortunately, the first Man abdicated his responsibilities as king and surrendered to the Adversary. Later in the book of Genesis, the Man remained passive and inactive when his wife was seduced by a serpent to partake of a piece of fruit—the same fruit that had been forbidden by God (Gen 3:6). As a result of his sin, the Man lost his innocence, his garden, and to a certain extent, his throne. The Adversary that deceived man became the prince and god of the world (John 12:31; 2 Cor 4:4). Because of his sin, death passed upon all men (Rom 5:12).

But what we lost in Adam, we gain in Christ. Jesus, the second Adam, came to destroy the power of the devil (Heb 2:14). He freed man from the domination of the Adversary and liberated him from the dominion of death. Now Christ reigns supreme over both heaven and earth (Matt 28:18). Daniel writes,

> I saw in the night visions, and behold, with the clouds of heaven there came one like a son of man, and he came to the Ancient of Days and was presented before him. And to him was given dominion and glory and a kingdom, that all peoples, nations, and languages should serve him; his dominion is an everlasting dominion, which shall not pass away, and his kingdom one that shall not be destroyed.
> Dan 7:13-14

This Lord of Glory, King Jesus the Christ, shares His authority with those who call upon His name (2 Tim 2:12; Rev 20:6). We were made to be kings. In Christ, we have been re-born to rule as kings. We bring order and honor to our domains when we live as Sons of Dust, exercising our authority righteously and upholding our duties and obligations faithfully. We have been given a kingdom (Luke 12:32). Now Yahweh expects us to serve like kings.

9

A MATCH MADE IN HEAVEN

> Scarcely had I passed them when I found him whom my soul loves. I held him, and would not let him go until I had brought him into my mother's house, and into the chamber of her who conceived me.
>
> Song 3:4

One of the greatest challenges when discussing masculinity is centering the conversation on what it means to be a Man. More often than not, the entire subject is viewed by surveying the differences between the masculine and feminine. In that way, masculinity is defined primarily by what it is not. It is not soft; it is not feminine. Part of the confusion has been the result of the feminist movement itself. Coupled with that movement, the failure of men to aptly understand themselves contributed to the anti-feminine definition of masculinity. The feminine-versus-masculine false dichotomy has really muddied the waters of gender differences and relationships over the past two decades. We—the Sons of Dust—need to be adequately versed in what masculinity is and not simply what it is not. In the Eden narrative thus far, we've been shown positive masculinity. The Man, our initial predecessor, is a soulful collection of dust and has been taught that he is made for adventure, battle, and communion with God. The Man was born to be a king. He is passionate, creative, resilient, determined, committed, benevolent, intelligent, and gracious. He is—at least at this particular point in human history—the perfect embodiment of manliness. Such being the case, it should capture our attention that God chose to highlight something lacking in the Man so early in the story.

Even before the entrance of sin into the world, something wasn't quite right. Something was incomplete. In the last chapter, we watched as the Man exercised his regal authority and brought order and blessing to the animal kingdom. He bestowed names upon all of God's creatures. But there is more at play than the naming of the animals; God is drawing attention to something the Man lacks—a mate. Before a single creature is brought to the Man, Yahweh offers us some insight. He had a helper for the Man in mind all along.

> Then the LORD God said, "It is not good that the man should be alone; I will make him helper fit for him." ... But for Adam there was not found a helper fit for him. So the LORD God caused a deep sleep to fall upon the man, and while he slept took one of his ribs and closed up its place with flesh. And the rib that the LORD God had taken from the man He made into a woman and brought her to the man.
> Gen 2:18, 20-22

The text calls this final created being "the Woman" (Gen 2:22); we know her as Eve, the mother of all living (Gen 3:20). When God created the Woman, He provided a physical counterpoint to the Man—a helper that fit him. This match—truly a match made in heaven—shows that God's intention was for the Woman to complete the Man. The Man and the Woman were not adversaries or enemies; they were not incompatible. The Woman was created for the Man. She filled a position that another man or a beast could not fulfill. While femininity never bestows masculinity, a woman can bring out the best in a man.

Man Alone

Up to this point, all of God's creation had been labeled "good" (Gen 1:10, 12, 18, 21, 25). But the Man without the Woman was labeled "not good" (Gen 2:18). As the animals passed before the Man, he noticed that each had a mate. The narrator records, "But for Adam there was not found a helper fit for him" (Gen 2:20). The buck had his doe. Each boar had his sow. The heifers were paired with their bulls. But there was not a mate for the Man.

God created the Man with a desire to love, protect, and provide, yet the first man had no one to shower with adoration, keep safe from harm, or bring his bacon home to. Let's revisit a quote from Eldridge that we used earlier:

> There are three desires I find written so deeply into my heart I know now I can no longer disregard them without losing my soul … In the heart of every man is a desperate desire for a battle to fight, an adventure to live, and a beauty to rescue.

That last one—"a beauty to rescue"—was absent before God's gracious creation of the Woman. The warrior needed someone to fight for. The king needed a queen. The Man needed someone who was his equal intellectually, spiritually, and personally but was unique, different, and special. The Man was incomplete without the Woman.

I'll say that again—the Man was incomplete without the Woman. There's a part of our masculine brain that rejects that statement. We want to assert our independence. We don't want to rely upon anyone. We boast of completeness and self-reliance without the agency of another human being—even someone as incredible as a woman. Bly touches on this part of the male mentality when he references Layard.

> John Layard reports that one old tradition holds that a stone, while still attached to the mountainside or the bedrock, is female. It becomes a male stone when it is moved away from its quarry place and set up by itself..." Male," John Layard says, "symbolizes that which is set apart."

But the cold, hard, biblical truth is that masculinity needs femininity to be complete. God never intended for the Man to dwell in perpetual solitude. He intended for man to have a companion that was equal but different from himself. But why? In the narrative of Gen 2 the answer is fairly basic. The Man needed the Woman for procreation. "Be fruitful and multiply and fill the earth" (Gen 1:28). That's what God would tell the newly united couple. But I suppose God could have created either the Man with the capability to reproduce asexually without the agency of a woman at all. Why then did God choose to make them male and female (Gen 1:27)?

Without presupposing too much, we can know that God created them male and female, masculine and feminine, for a particular purpose. God made the Woman to better the Man (1 Cor 11:9). The Woman didn't improve the Man through nagging, domineering, or correcting his faux pas. She was, as Eldridge states, "someone to fight for." In his book, *The Code of Man*, Newell writes,

> The wisdom of the West about erotic relations between men and women can be summed up in a single maxim: Love perfects ... A man's love for a woman can give him the strongest possible motive to overcome his own vices in order to prove himself worthy of her.

"Love perfects." All that God had instilled in the Man would be brought into focus, honed, and utilized in his relationship with his wife. Men have always been brought to their full potential when fighting to protect their women. We think of the ancient Spartan men who marched off to war—though vastly outnumbered—against the Persians to preserve their way of life and protect their women and children. The Greatest Generation defeated the Axis Powers in their service to a woman—Lady Liberty. Jesus Christ Himself was perfected through His suffering (Heb 2:10), suffering He underwent for the benefit of His bride—the church (Eph 5:25-27). Through his relationship with his wife, the Man would be actively and progressively improved as an individual. The same takes place in the lives of the Sons of Dust. Whether by marriage to a godly woman or marriage to Christ, we are motivated by our love and the love shown toward us to become more and more like Jesus Christ.

As we actively, sacrificially, and completely love our wives, we are replicating Jesus and His love for the church.

A Fit Helper

Twice the narrator makes the comment that God would construct "a helper fit for" the Man (Gen 2:18, 20). Yahweh did not intend to make a second creature just like the first. He did not desire one exactly like the Man. Instead, God determined to make the perfect pair—the Man encapsulating all the traits that God desired in him, and the Woman possessing the qualities of the feminine. Like two adjoining puzzle pieces, the Woman was to be the compliment to the Man. She was similar but not the same, and she would be exactly what he needed.

The concept of a "helper" is interesting in light of other biblical passages. The term is used to refer to both divine assistance—God helping His people—or military aid (Isa 30:5; Ezek 12:14; Hos 13:9). When such texts are considered and connected with the Genesis narrative, it's easy for us to understand just how vital the Woman's role was in relationship to the Man. The feminine counterpart would be a helper in the utmost sense of the word; she would provide assistance and aid that contributed to the Man's success. In all his endeavors—his physical, mental, emotional, and spiritual development, as well as the achieving of his God-given purpose—she would support him and propel him to higher accomplishments. The LORD did not create the Man's helper to be a perpetual thorn in his side. Far from it, in fact. She would be the best compliment to his form and character. The Woman would be his life-saver.

The Woman would also be a helper *fit* for him. Notice that she was not chosen by the Man. He did not scour singles' sites or seedy bars to find a bride that met his own whims. This woman—the Woman—was created by God to be the perfect match for the Man. To be "fit for him" means that the Woman was the "like opposite of him." In many ways, she was his mirror image—a partner that was equal in every way, but endowed wherein he was lacking. To summarize the entire concept: the Man and the Woman were complimentary. I do not mean that he lavished her with praise, though he certainly did. They were complimentary in the sense that he was what she was not, and she was what he was not. He was male. She was female. He was masculine. She was feminine. The one completed and complimented the other. Of Gen 1-2, Stenson and Dumas write,

> The creation account in Genesis 1 reveals the shared work God gave men and women to do—He created mankind as male and female and tasked them both to take dominion, to subdue the earth and to be fruitful. The next two chapters of Genesis however, provide additional details about the creation of mankind; showing how men and women who are equal in essence, are distinct in function in how they fulfill the tasks God gave them in a complementary way.

The fact that masculinity and femininity are complementary one to another should give sufficient reason for meditation. "Complimentary" does not mean that masculinity and femininity are mutually exclusive. The best men have embodied characteristics that are classically referred to as feminine qualities. Winston Churchill, the Lion of London, loved to paint and express himself creatively.

Likewise, honorable women have possessed certain masculine traits. Need we mention Joan of Ark or Deborah of biblical fame? As we've already stated, masculine means more than simply "not feminine." What God is implying here is that masculinity is maintained, expressed, and best seen when combined with the feminine—not when masculinity is contrasted against it. The two are not at odds one with another; masculinity and femininity blend to create a complete tapestry of humanity. The ultimate combination of the two takes place in a God-centered marriage between a man and his wife.

The Husband's Role

I can remember going under the knife when I was seventeen-years-old. Well, I can remember the preparations that preceded my operation. By the time the scalpel touched the skin, I was fully sedated. I remember talking with the anesthesiologist prior to surgery. The Bible is filled with a lot of first, but who knew that God was the first anesthesiologist? "So the LORD God cause a deep sleep to fall upon the Man, and while he slept took one of his is and closed up its place with flesh" (Gen 2:21). This deep sleep was divinely induced (Isa 29:10; 1 Sam 26:12), but the slumber isn't the main focus of the passage. While the Man was napping, God took a piece of flesh from his side.

It is from this piece of flesh from the side of the Man that God built a woman. "And the rib that the LORD God had taken from the man, He made into a woman and brought her to the man" (Gen 2:22). Of all the comments ever made about the creation of woman, Matthew Henry's reigns supreme: "The woman was made of a rib out of the side of Adam; not made out of his head to rule over him, nor out of his feet to be trampled upon by him, but out of his side to be equal with him, under his arm to be protected, and near his heart to be beloved." The Woman was made from the side of the Man. Therein lies a wonderful picture of the type of relationship God intended for the Man and his wife to possess.

Simply put, the Man is to be the provider and protector of his wife. These are the same two roles that God placed under the Man's control when God placed him in the garden in Eden "to work it and to keep it" (Gen 2:15). Just as man provided what was necessary for the creation of woman—a piece of rib meat—Yahweh intended for a man to serve his wife as her provider. Since she was literally the byproduct of his own flesh, "Husbands should love their wives as their own bodies" (Eph 5:28). Though we are several thousand miles and several thousand years removed from the garden in Eden, our roles and responsibilities toward our wives have not been diminished at all. "If anyone does not provide for his relatives, and especially for members of his household, he has denied the faith and is worse than an unbeliever" (1 Tim 5:8). Husbands are to provide for their wives physically, support their wives emotionally (Eph 5:29), and lead their wives spiritually (1 Pet 3:7). Sons of Dust are both benevolent and providing kings and defending warriors.

God's Hierarchy

We've already stated that the Man did not chose his own bride. The marriage of the first couple was an arranged marriage. The LORD God was in the interesting position of being the Progenitor of both the bride and the groom. God "brought her to the Man" (Gen 2:22). The rabbis taught that God acted as the best man on this occasion. The action of bringing the Woman to the Man implies that God is placing the crown of His creation in the care of the Man. She would be subject to him.

Just as men naturally balk at any hint of our dependence upon another person, many women will decry subjection to man. Most will hail from the camps of radical feminists. Some will be innocent recipients of tainted information touted by some from the same movement. However, there is a hierarchy laid down in Genesis that can be traced throughout the rest of the Bible. God—as the King that He is—has instituted a divine order that is to be respected.

Paul says, "But I want you to understand that the head of every man is Christ, the head of a wife is her husband, and the head of Christ is God" (1 Cor 11:3). Wives are told to "submit in everything to their husbands" (Eph 5:24). The husband is the head of the house like Christ is the head of the church (Eph 5:23). Some will say that such a hierarchy is patriarchal, antiquated, and not applicable in modern society; however, when Paul was directed of the Spirit to discuss God's design for both the home and the church, he couched his argument by returning all the way to the beginning.

> Let a woman learn quietly with all submissiveness. I do not permit a woman to teach or to exercise authority over a man; rather, she is to remain quiet. For Adam was formed first, then Eve; and Adam was not deceived, but the woman was deceived and became a transgressor.
>
> 1 Tim 2:11-14

It is God's intention that men lead, provide, and direct based upon supreme love—a love like Christ had for His church. It is God's desire for wives to submit to their own husbands, honoring and respecting him for his office's sake.

* * *

Much of what it means to be masculine cannot be understood without considering femininity. Newell is right: "Women are sometimes the best authorities on the meaning of manliness." When we encounter real femininity like that found in the first woman, Sons of Dust are reminded of what God has called them to be—providers and protectors. Masculinity and femininity are not opposed or contradictory; instead, they are a match made in heaven.

10

THE FIRST POET

> Because your steadfast love is better than life, my lips will praise you.
>
> Ps 63:3

I can remember the first time I saw Her. Chances are you can as well. She was radiant and beautiful, capable of capturing your attention with only a passing glance. It might have been her hair, her eyes, or her form; it could have been her voice, her laugh, or even her scent. Odysseus heard her siren song while sailing the Mediterranean. David watched her bathe on the roof of a house in Jerusalem (2 Sam 11:2). Paris, the prince of Troy, kidnapped her and started the Trojan War. A certain American president found her serving as a White House intern. All of these men—to one degree or another—saw the same thing that the first man saw. The Man, Adam, is the ultimate embodiment of God-created masculinity. The Woman—the one known to us as *Eve*—is the perfect counterpart to the Man. She was the prototypical woman. She embodied all that God created a woman to be—at least until the Fall. All that we find pleasurable, alluring, enticing, or lovable in a woman has its roots in Eve.

You don't have to tell any red-blooded male that there is something alluring about the feminine form. God intended for such to be the case. In creating a "helper fit" for the Man, God built the Woman to satisfy him and bring out the best in him. As stated in the previous chapter, God created the Woman to be the recipient of the protecting and providential love of the Man. Until the creation of the Woman, the Man's drive, passion, and focus had been centered upon tilling the ground, taking care of the garden, exploring the countryside, and dominating the earth. While each of these activities speak to our masculine heart, Yahweh wanted the Man to use everything at his disposal to tenderly care for another person. God created Eve to unlock the lover within every man. God intends for you to woo and romance. On an even deeper level, the LORD made you to enjoy the intricacies of life that draw us into a deeper relationship with Him—sunrises, sunsets, sonnets, and sonatas.

When we get a good glimpse of distilled femininity, we can sense a little of what the Man felt when God introduced him to his woman. The moment the Man's eyes fell upon the form of his bride his lips burst forth in praise. God took the opportunity to provide further insight about the joys of monogamous marriage.

> Then the man said, "This at last is bone of my bones and flesh of my flesh; she shall be called Woman, because she was taken out of Man." Therefore a man shall leave his father and his mother and hold fast to his wife, and they shall become one flesh.
>
> Gen 2:23-24

These two verses encapsulate the emotion of the lover placed by God within every man. Sons of Dust need to look deep within themselves and search for the passionate, playful, and expressive soul that God has placed there—the same soul He placed within the Man. This spirit placed within man is for more than romantic relationships with special women. This heart unlocks the rich and deep emotional experiences life has to offer. Speaking of this aspect of our nature, Moore and Gillette write,

> We believe that the Lover, by whatever name, is the primal energy pattern of what we could call vividness, aliveness, and passion. It lives through the great primal hungers of our species for sex, food, well-being, reproduction, creative adaptation to life's hardships, and ultimately a sense of meaning, without which human beings cannot go on with their lives. The Lover's drive is to satisfy those hungers.

Many men have been accused of being too logical, too stoic, or too unemotional. Chances are those men have failed to understand the nature of the masculine heart that God placed in the first Man. Yahweh intends for us to feel and to react to feelings, to love and respond of love.

The First Poem

I've never fancied myself as a poet. Furthermore, I'm not musically inclined or a particularly talented lyricist. Some men are—and you may be one such man. I am not. But there are certain aspects of my nature that were unlocked when in the presence of incredible beauty. When I met the woman who now is my wife, she introduced me to a world of passion and romance previously hidden from my gaze. You've felt it—colors and shades become more radiant, each note of a song is pregnant with poignancy, and smells are more enticing. My Eve stirred my heart and resurrected a part of my nature that had been dormant. Even after several years of marriage, her love motivates me to write, play music, and enjoy "the finer things in life."

When I think about our wedding, I feel remarkably close to my earliest ancestor—the Man in the narrative of Gen 2. I can still feel the ocean breeze blowing against the back of my neck, the sound of whipping wind encircling my earlobes. I could smell the salt and—at least I imagine now—the gentle scent of the rose petals strewn on the beach. The music and the crash of the waves see-sawed in ambient volume. Then, after moments of waiting, I saw her waltzing down the boardwalk and descending the stairs toward the beach. She slid her shoes off and began to walk barefooted down the beach towards me. Her eyes met mine, and I could see the subtle mixture of blues, greens, and grays that I had come to adore. A smile spread across her face. Her hair—the particularly dark shade of taupe—was pulled back to reveal her royal features. I held her soft, slender hands and listened to her voice over the din of the ocean. After the officiant concluded his presentation, I held my Melissa Jane, ensconced with bliss, adoration, and rapturous love. Though I did not have the presence of mind or the wherewithal to couch my thoughts in harmonic language, the entire proceeding left me feeling poetic, alive, and sensitive to all the beauty of life. The best love will do that.

When the Man beheld his wife for the first time, the experience moved him to poetic expression. The narrator presents the statement of the Man in its true form—the first expression of poetry. Man's first creation was not a garden, structure, or even a piece of pottery. As incredible as it may seem, the first thing ever made by man was a poem. The Man was the first poet. His four lines illuminate the heart of the lover God placed within his breasts. He speaks of longing and satisfaction, origin and completion. The first expression to emerge from the poet's lips speaks of his intense longing for a mate—"This at last!" He was incomplete, lacking, and un-whole. He had been unable to find a mate in the rest of creation; no animals—fish, fowl, beast, or creeping thing—could satisfy the longing of his heart. Finally, the LORD had found a helper suitable for him.

His feeling of relief and joy blended with the soft tenderness of fellow-feeling and sympathy in its truest sense—"This at last is bone of my bones and flesh of my flesh." The Woman was truly made from the flesh of the Man. She was made from his own essence, but she was profoundly different and complementary in form. Nothing is said of childrearing, for the Woman is valued for who she is alone and not her practical benefits. The Man is connected, joined, and united with a being like himself.

In an act of protective authority, the Man bestows a name upon his new companion—"She shall be called 'Ishah, because she was taken out of 'Ish." He does not call her Eve, at least not yet (Gen 3:20). Now she is only "the Woman," a term meaning simply "the female of the man." The Man is connecting the Woman with himself. She was called "maleness," for she was taken from the male. Both the Man and the Woman were intricately connected, tied to one another by creation, experience, and future opportunities.

Sons of Dust need to channel the lover placed by God within the heart of man. We need to learn how to woo, how to romance, and how to connect with the emotional aspect of our own nature in a helpful and beneficial way.

More needs to be said about romancing our wives. Learn to woo her. Learn to make her swoon. "Live with your wives in an understanding way" (1 Pet 3:7) and nourish and cherish her. Sing to her. Walk with her. Look longingly upon both her body and spirit. Learn to make her feel valuable and desirable just as Christ did for His church (Eph 5:29). As Newell said, "For a man to see himself through a woman's eyes, and to imagine how he might appall or amuse her, is the real beginning of growing up." Loving a woman is one of the most sincere forms of adventure. As Eldridge says, "The adventure begins and our real strength is released when we no longer rely on formulas." The lover sets aside the facts and the figures for the figure of a woman—or the Woman.

God Designed Marriage

The Man, the lover responsible for the poetic expression of Gen 2:23, would need the same lover's heart to fulfill his roles and responsibilities as a husband. Too many men see the value of romantic expression while dating or courting, but hasten to exchange the warmth of the rose for tepid reason soon after marriage. The life, vitality, and emotion encapsulated within the breast of the Man would only come to be more fully expressed through the practice of marriage. The contemporary crisis in masculinity has led to a deterioration in the modern American marriage. Something has malfunctioned, and we need to get things back to working order. God gave His own stamp of approval upon marriage after the Man's poetic vows. He takes the implications of the Man's speech and applies them to every marriage that would ever be consummated. Though there is much talk of the love and marriage in modern society, little of God's original intention is considered.

The LORD God intends for a man and his wife to start a new family. He states, "Therefore a man shall leave his father and his mother" (Gen 2:24). Independence from one's parents is actively declared by marriage, if not before. The apron strings must be cut; a husband's dependance on mother and father should be set aside and forever abandoned. The lover is not to be guided by the guises and whims of his parents; his heart is devoted to his beloved and to her alone. A man begins a new family when he takes a wife. Their union is one that is divinely originated and supremely blessed. A husband becomes the king of a newly formed nation—a dominion of two. He is to be the king of his castle and to rule his home with humility and grace, independent from the home of his father.

There is also permanence and loyalty in marriage. God instructs the Man to "hold fast to his wife, and they shall become one flesh" (Gen 2:24). A man is to be glued to his wife, bound in a union that will last to death (1 Cor 7:39). In the narrative in Genesis, there is no mention of divorce or separation, for neither was contained in God's original plan for marriage. Jesus says, "Moses allowed you to divorce your wives, but from the beginning it was not so" (Matt 19:8). Though it may take determination, it is the heart of the lover who remains committed to his wife. He forsakes all others and remains faithful to his spouse so long as they both are living.

The heart of the lover revels in the passion of marriage. A man and his wife are "one flesh." A couple experiences a union stronger and deeper than a blood relationship, for they have been knit together by God. The souls of two lovers cleave to one another (Gen 34:3), united in a bond that only death can destroy.

The maintenance of a faithful marriage is impossible without the fixed determination of a dedicated lover. The Man would need to be active and engaged. A lover longs for interaction with his beloved. Modern marriages are enriched as often as they are visited by the lover placed within every man. We must, as Bly writes, choose that "one precious thing" and be willing to devote our entire being to loving another.

A Word of Warning

When we speak of loving or of being a lover, we do not mean that the central focus of a man's love should be a woman. Biblical men recognize that God has called us to love Him with all that our nature possesses (Mark 12:30). However, the mistake made by the Man in the Genesis narrative has been made by countless men throughout history. Eldridge saw the Man's downfall when he wrote, "Eve took the place of God in a man's life." When it came time for the Man to resist temptation, he caved. He loved Eve and the temptation she put before him more than he loved God. When we appreciate beauty—whether the form of a flower or a woman—we should be motivated to love and adore God. Eldridge says again,

> What else is it we are seeking from the Woman with the Golden Hair? What is that ache we are trying to assuage with her? ... in a word, God. I'm serious. What we are looking for is God.

Why? Because the lover really wants to connect himself with God. Yahweh expressed his love through the creation of the perfect counterpart for the Man. That woman caused the Man to erupt in poetry, for she was a physical manifestation of God's love for the Man. David knew and experienced this interconnection of love, a love for the creation and the Creator. He uses language that almost makes us blush, even when speaking of God (Psa 63:2-8). Jesus, the Son of God, was both loved by God and expressed His love for God (John 14:31). This heavenly love was expressed in His relationship with others as well (John 15:9). Because He loved the Father and the Father loved Him, Jesus was capable of communicating the riches of emotional love with His own disciples. Real, lasting love is experienced when the lover connects his own love for God with his love for another human being. Thus did Christ. Thus did Adam.

We need to exercise caution when exploring the lover, for we can easily be led astray by that which we find beautiful. When a young man experiences the blazing flame of lust, he would do well to remember Bly's counsel.

> What does it mean when a man falls in love with a radiant face across the room? It may mean that he has some soul work to do. He soul is the issue. Instead of pursuing the woman and trying to get her alone, away from her husband, he needs to go alone himself, perhaps to a mountain cabin, for three months, write poetry, canoe down a river, and dream. That would save some women a lot of trouble.

Those of us who are wed should love our wives passionately and without regret. We should sacrifice for her and serve her. We should honor and cherish her. But at the same time, we should thank God for her blessing and give God the praise for her grace. We should allow her beauty to draw us into a deeper union with Him. Thus did Christ. Thus did Adam.

11

HAVE YOU NO SHAME?

> Those who look to him are radiant, and their faces shall never be ashamed.
>
> Ps 34:5

We are over six thousand years removed from the paradise in Eden. The geography, topography, and climate of the earth has changed significantly. Republics, monarchies, and empires have ascended to power and vanished from the earth. We've exchanged shovels and hoes for diesel cultivators and combines. Fig leaves and coats of skins have long been replaced by wools and synthetics. However, one thing still remains the same. Eldridge writes, "If a boy is to become a man, if a man is to know he is one, this is not an option. A man has to know where he comes from, and what he's made of." We were made from the dust. We were designed by God and endowed with the traits we associate with manliness—honor, courage, temperance, passion, and strength. We were made to glorify God, having been created in His image and entrusted with the dominion of the earth. We are descendants of the Man. We are Sons of Dust.

We've meditated upon the words given by the Holy Spirit through the pen of Moses. The narrator presents the proto-man in all his glory. The Man is created by the LORD God—the powerful Being who began by creating all things and chose to make a covenant with man. This God stoops to the earth, collects dirt within His hand, and forms the Man. He breathes upon him as a ancient blacksmith blows upon coals and causes the Man to become a living soul. The Man is a farmer. He is charged with tilling the ground and sharing in the work of Yahweh. He is a warrior, for he alone will protect all that is in the garden from harm. He is spiritual and intelligent, entering into a covenant relationship with his God that demands his fealty and obedience. He is given freedom to explore, conquer, and experience all that God has created for his enjoyment. The Man is a king, a ruler over all the earth, who is in need of a queen. The LORD graciously builds a helper complimentary to the Man to rule and reign with him. Beneath it all, the Man has the heart of a lover—a heart that will delight in his wife, his God, and all things beautiful. The Man, as he is presented in the second chapter of Genesis, is pure, perfect, and lacking nothing.

> And the Man and his wife were both naked and were not ashamed.
>
> Gen 2:25

The narrator closes the story of the creation of mankind with an astonishing claim. Both the Man and his bride were naked and stood in the presence of God, yet neither of them felt shame or guilt. The Man does not seek to cover his nakedness. He does not cower or retreat from the presence of his bride. He basks in the light of the sun and in the light of God's glorious radiance. He is masculine. He is manly. He is not ashamed.

Our Shame

It is hard for us to comprehend this type of shamelessness. We cover our bodies with clothing in an attempt to hide all our imperfections. We conceal the deepest thoughts and feelings of our hearts by remaining silent or discussing shallow topics like sports, the weather, or automobiles. We avoid examining our faults or admitting our shortcomings. For almost every man, there is something that overshadows his life with guilt. Eldridge, Bly, and others call this shame or guilt "a wound." Something deep within our hearts has been wounded or harmed, and this scar moves us to shame.

Sometimes this wound is self-inflicted. Such was the case with the Man in the Genesis account. He chose to partake of the fruit of the tree of knowledge and commit sin before God. His sin brought shame upon him. He wounded himself (Gen 3:6-10). Doubtless, our sin is self-inflicted as well. We have chosen to rebel against God. "All we like sheep have gone astray" (Isa 53:6). We have sinned (Rom 3:23). We are guilty, whether we see it or not (John 9:41). But for those of use who are Sons of Dust, we have been redeemed by the blood of Jesus (Rev 1:5). Our sin, guilt, and shame has been removed (Rom 5:5). We are no longer guilty, for we have been forgiven. Since we have been forgiven and bear no guilt, we should no longer carry shame (1 Pet 2:6).

Why then do so many men still feel ashamed? Why are we afraid or self-conscious? Those who have been forgiven may still bear scars from a wound inflicted by another—a father, a wife, a teacher, or a friend. For whatever reason, someone has convinced us that we don't have what it takes. We hide our masculinity and place a cardboard cut-out of stereotypical male ego in its stead. We are ashamed of who we are—who we were created to be.

In spite of those who have whispered, "You don't have what it takes," we have been assured by a loving Father that He has redeemed us and that He delights in us (Rom 8:14-17). He firmly places His hand upon our shoulders and says, "You are more than a conqueror. You are my son."

The Man stood in the presence of God and was not ashamed, because he embodied all that God intended for him to be. Sons of Dust who call upon God and have been initiated into mature manhood can stand before God with pride and confidence, secure in their masculinity because they are secure in Christ. We will never perfectly embody biblical manliness, but as we are constantly being initiated by God, we are being conformed into the image of One Who was the perfect image of masculinity—Jesus Christ (Rom 8:29). As we allow God to work in and through us, He cultivates the masculine heart that He has already placed there. Those who belong to Christ have no reason to be ashamed.

You are a warrior, a king, a lover, an explorer, and a son of God. That is what Yahweh has created you to be. There is no need for you to feel shame or guilt for possessing the qualities associated with mature biblical masculinity. Even secular writers like Moore and Gillette recognize that the world needs more real men—"In the present crisis in masculinity we do not need, as some feminists are saying, less masculine power. We need more."

Sons of Dust are able to stand bravely in the presence of God. They are able to stand under the adoring gaze of their wives without shyness or fear, knowing they are lovingly and sacrificially serving her through their masculinity. They are confident and assured because they are being made whole by God.

A World of Opposition

"We live in a world of counterfeits," says Eldridge, "counterfeit battles, counterfeit adventures, counterfeit beauties." I would add that the world is filled with counterfeit men—those who strut through life flaunting an inflated and insincere form of masculinity. The counterfeit masculinity known to the world is completely at odds with biblical manliness. Just as the secular world has no place for Adam, they have little room for his sons. Do not be deceived. It will not be easy to live a life of biblical manliness; it will not be simple to live as a Son of Dust. Listen to what Jesus said on the eve of His own crucifixion:

> If the world hates you, know that it has hated me before it hated you. If you were of the world, the world would love you as its own; but because you are not of the world, but I chose you out of the world, therefore the world hates you. Remember the word that I said to you: "A servant is not greater than his master." If they persecuted me, they will also persecute you. If they kept my word, they will also keep yours. But all these things they will do to you on account of my name, because they do not know him who sent me.
>
> John 15:18-21

And again:

> I have said all these things to you to keep you from falling away. They will put you out of the synagogues. Indeed, the hour is coming when whoever kills you will think he is offering service to God. And they will do these things because they have not known the Father, nor me. But I have said these things to you, that when their hour comes you may remember that I told them to you.
>
> John 16:1-4

Jesus foretold that the world would reject His followers just as the world rejected Him. But why did the world reject Christ? The world rejected the Second Adam because they preferred the course of the First Adam. They chose sin over the Savior and autonomy over submission. They refused to accept the only True Man who has ever lived upon the earth. Nevertheless, Christ was not defeated or deterred from His mission, and He did not intend for His disciples to be.

> I have said these things to you, that in me you may have peace. In the world you will have tribulation. But take heart; I have overcome the world.
>
> John 16:33

Your Challenge

Where do we go from here? The world is in desperate need of real men—men who have been initiated by God into the fullness of what He intended masculinity to be. Sons of Dust must allow themselves to be conformed to Christ and, thereby, to be reunited with Adam—the Man of the Genesis narrative. We must see the world in which we live as a ripe opportunity, ready for the influence of true masculinity. Our homes, churches, communities, and even our nation is ready for the entrance of the Sons of Dust. We need an understanding of our own nature and dependance upon God, for He alone is able to bring about the change we desperately need.

God is calling for the Sons of Dust to be warriors capable of defending our souls and the souls of those around us. He is rallying those who have been freed from the dominion of the devil and is granting them positions of authority in His kingdom to reign with His Son. Yahweh needs passionate, engaged men who are in love with their own wives, with the Lord, and with His bride—the church. The clarion call resounding in the hearts of men is for male leadership that is not ashamed of its own maleness, but is qualified, prepared, and steady enough for the hardships awaiting them in service unto Christ.

Your family, your church, your land, and your Lord are all asking the same thing of you. Live like the the Man that God has created you to be. Live as one of the Sons of Dust.

ACKNOWLEDGMENTS

There are so many to whom I owe a great depth of gratitude for their influence and support of this project. I never imaged that I would be allowed to write a book, but I am thankful to God for giving me the opportunity to do so. With that opportunity, He also provided a cast of supporters, encouragers, and friends to help me see it through to completion.

First, I owe more than my life to my beautiful bride, Melissa Jane. She has given me over to the writing of this book for several months and has selflessly allowed me to work early, late, alone, and away in order to complete it. She has helped me to see the beauty and glory of God more than any other person and has used her femininity to increase my own masculinity. All that she is as a woman has bettered me as a man. She is my muse, my love, and my greatest encourager. I love you with all my heart, Melissa Jane.

My parents are to be thanked for their contribution to my life. My mother's early guidance and my father's counsel have enriched my life beyond measure. I am thankful for their faithfulness. I love you, Moms and Pops.

Josh, Kristin, and Jessica—my siblings—have always encouraged and loved me. May God bless you all. I love you.

My grandparents—Nanny and Pa, Mema and Poppy, Grandmomma and Grandaddy—are worthy of thanks. Thank you for your encouragement and all the wonderful memories I have shared with you. Your legacy will never be forgotten.

Cliff Goodwin, Tom Holland, Keith Mosher, and Jim Murrell have guided me as a preacher and teacher and have provided so much wisdom and strength to my life.

Trent Webster, Robert Hatfield, Brad McNutt, Torrey Clark, Josh Manning, Dwayne Butler, Wesley Skelton, and Michael Whitworth have been my brothers-in-arms. I am thankful to stand beside them. "Once more into the fray..."

I dare not list all the younger men whom I cherish and pray for regularly. They have a wealth of potential and hearts ready for service in the army of my Lord. They know who they are. I love you all as an elder brother.

My special thanks is offered to Bill Camp, a faithful friend and brother in Christ, who has shown me a heart of devotion—both to his wife and to our Father in heaven. His prayers, books, and wisdom mean more to me than most else in life. I truly love you, brother Camp.

More than all others, my God and Father, the Lord Jesus Christ, and the Spirit of God are worthy of my eternal praise, adoration, and thanks. May all the glory gained from the writing and circulation of this book be given to them.

WORKS CITED

The Code of Man by Waller R. Newell

A Guide to Biblical Manhood by Randy Stinson and Dan Dumas

Iron John: A Book About Men by Robert Bly

King, Warrior, Magician, Lover: Rediscovering the Archetypes of the Mature Masculine by Robert Moore and Doug Gillette

The Strenuous Life by Theodore Roosevelt

Wild At Heart by John Eldridge

The Way of the Wild Heart by John Eldridge

www.ingramcontent.com/pod-product-compliance
Lightning Source LLC
Chambersburg PA
CBHW071212070526
44584CB00019B/3009